FOR THE LOVE OF TREES

A Guide to the Trees of Ottawa's Central Experimental Farm Arboretum

Richard Hinchcliff and Roman Popadiouk

Photographs by Richard Hinchcliff
Illustrations by Karen (Gier) Cameron

Library and Archives Canada Cataloguing in Publication

For the love of trees / Roman Popadiouk and Richard Hinchcliff.

ISBN 978-1-897113-73-8

1. Trees—Ontario—Ottawa—Pictorial works. 2. Trees—Ontario—Ottawa—
Identification. 3. Dominion Arboretum and Botanic Garden of Canada—
Guidebooks. I. Hinchcliff, Richard, 1943- II. Title.
QK480.C32D64 2007   582.1609713'84   C2007-903359-8

Published by:
General Store Publishing House
499 O'Brien Road, Box 415, Renfrew, Ontario, Canada K7V 4A6
1-800-465-6072   www.gsph.com

Project Chair: Valerie Cousins
Editor: Rosaleen Leslie Dickson
Text Review: Karen (Gier) Cameron, Liz Brittain
Science: Roman Popadiouk
Photographs, History: Richard Hinchcliff
Illustrations: Karen (Gier) Cameron, except p.111 by Valerie Cousins
Fund Raising: Richard Conway, Valerie Cousins
Scientific Review: Ken Farr, Gisèle Mitrow, Joan Speirs
Design: Alison R. Hall, Design en Plus
Printing: Tri-Graphic Printing (Ottawa) Limited

The Friends of the Farm gratefully acknowledges the financial support of:

The City of Ottawa

The Harold Crabtree Foundation

E. Neville Ward in memory of his mother Kathleen Elizabeth Ward

Front cover, top, left to right: Scarlet Oak, Black Locust, Ponderosa Pine; bottom, path by the old Windbreak.
Back cover, top, left to right: Bebb's Oak, Scots Pine, 'Chilko' Crab Apple; middle, Red Maple.
Title pages: Yellow Buckeye (drawing), Sycamore, Manitoba Maple.
Opposite: Cutleaf Norway Maple.

ACKNOWLEDGEMENTS

This book would not exist without **Valerie Cousins**. It was her idea, and it was her inspiration and leadership that made it happen. Her artistic and communications skills, and her love for the Farm, have influenced all aspects of the project. Thanks to Valerie, it has indeed been a celebration.

Our thanks to **Karen (Gier) Cameron** for her beautiful tree silhouettes and the hours of painstaking work involved. Her ideas, illustrations and draft text for the glossary, text reviews, and collection of specimens to photograph were also much appreciated.

The splendid look of the book, including the maps, is thanks to **Alison Hall** of Design en Plus. As soon as she showed us her first page design, we began to believe the book was going to work. Our thanks to her also for managing the production of the book.

Many thanks to **Rosaleen Dickson** for her expert editing, to **Richard Conway** for his fundraising, and to **Liz Brittain** for her reviews and helpful comments. Thanks also to **Doug Shouldice** and **Judy Benner** for their help and encouragement, and to **Dorothy Forsyth** for her support in our fundraising.

We are grateful to **E. Neville Ward** and his mother **Kathleen Elizabeth Ward**, centenarian (1906-2006). She loved trees, especially those in the Arboretum, and often stated how lucky we are to have the Arboretum in the centre of Ottawa.

Scientific review was kindly provided by **Ken Farr**, **Gisèle Mitrow** and **Joan Speirs**. Special thanks to Joan, lilac specialist for the Friends of the Farm, for her help on the Japanese Tree Lilac.

We pay tribute to the many teams of dedicated staff who have worked over the years to make and keep the Arboretum such a special place. Many thanks to the team at Agriculture and Agri-Food Canada, including **Pierre Huppé**, **Brian Douglas**, **Sharon Saunders**, and **Jean-Pascal Gratton**, for their help while this book was being prepared.

AAFC and staff, our designer, editor and scientific reviewers bear no responsibility for any errors or inadequacies with this book. Those are ours.

Finally, we thank **Josephine Stanic** and **Galina Ponomarenko** for their patience and support.

Richard Hinchcliff and Roman Popadiouk

Contents

FOREWORD *by Marjorie Harris*

Trees are Canada's greatest resource. We think of them as endlessly renewable but we are learning that they are as fragile as any other part of our ecosystem. We could spend dozens of years studying nothing else and still they would be a mystery to us. And yet we have massively abused these plants.

Complex and paradoxical, trees provide us with a living, yet on a general scale we know almost nothing about them. They grow, therefore we exploit them. When the first Europeans arrived on these shores all they could see was huge masts. What a bonanza for a people who'd long since logged out most of their own countries or had nature do it for them with climate change in the Little Ice Age.

Climate change is once again with us, but now as we all know with much more terrifying results. It should tell us that we must value every tree on this planet. The Central Experimental Farm Arboretum in Ottawa is one of our best, most convincing resources in appreciating these great plants. It brings us to a greater understanding of trees and their ecosystems, and makes a subtle demand for their survival.

This wonderful book calls attention to some of the loveliest trees in our forests. Many of them are native trees, others were brought to this country by our ancestors. From ornamental to resource to food trees, there is an articulate mix here that will inform and enchant any reader. The information is so clearly laid out in this book, it will become invaluable to anyone who knows and loves a tree.

Marjorie Harris is editor-at-large of "Gardening Life" magazine; garden columnist for the "Globe and Mail"; and author of many books including *Botanica North America* and *How to Make a Garden: The 7 Essential Steps for Canadian Gardeners.*

A Work of Love

For those of us who grew up in Ottawa, the Central Experimental Farm was an important playground. Throughout the year there was always a reason to visit the Farm — newly born lambs, fragrance of the lilac collection in spring, boats on Dow's Lake and the canal in summer, autumn foliage, and tobogganing in winter. Having a thousand acres of fields, gardens and an arboretum as a place to frolic was simply the norm for us.

Only as we grew older did it dawn on us what a rare gem this picturesque historic landscape was, right in the middle of our growing city. The best gift was the Arboretum, with its rolling hills, high lookouts, water views and of course the spectacular trees! Our children have experienced many of the same thrills as we did at the Arboretum, which continues to attract thousands of visitors every year. Newcomers to Canada love the Farm too, finding some of the common elements that make a city a home — beauty and quiet, the sky and the trees, a safe place to wonder and ponder.

It is therefore no surprise that we would want to be part of a volunteer organization — Friends of the Farm — that works to preserve, enhance and protect the Farm. It is no surprise that we would want to publish a book that celebrates the Arboretum and its precious tree collections, their history and their science. We wanted a book that would profile the unique trees in the collection and capture the exquisite beauty of the trees and vistas.

We hope this book will be a source of beauty and learning for all who visit the Arboretum or love trees. In many ways, it is our love song to the trees and we hope it will be yours as well, for many generations to come.

Doug Shouldice, President, Friends of the Farm
Valerie Cousins, Chair, Publishing Team and Past President,
Friends of the Farm
September 2007

" *(The Arboretum) is separated by a public road from the main part of the Farm; and is most beautifully situated on a high bank overlooking the canal; being laid out with winding roads and seeded down with grass, it will in a year or two present the aspect of a lovely park which will doubtless be much frequented by visitors."*

SARAH AGNES SAUNDERS,
THE OTTAWA EVENING JOURNAL, APRIL 13, 1895

A NATIONAL TREASURE

"...encouragement has been given to the planting of trees, shrubs and flowers so that our people might surround themselves with objects of beauty, the study and observance of which will refine their minds and add quiet enjoyment to their lives." WILLIAM SAUNDERS, FIRST DIRECTOR OF CANADA'S EXPERIMENTAL FARM SYSTEM, 1896

The Arboretum in Ottawa, Canada's capital, is a green space of 26 hectares (64 acres), just minutes from the centre of the city. It is part of the more than 400 hectare (1,000 acre) Central Experimental Farm that has been called the lungs of the city. Many of the estimated 175,000 visitors who enjoy the peace and pathways of the Arboretum each year may not be aware that it is home to a unique collection of trees representing a legacy of years of scientific research.

For the Love of Trees introduces the trees of 92 species, a small fraction of the more than 1,700 tree and shrub types in the Arboretum. An illustrated profile of each selected species is provided, with maps to show where the trees can be found.

THE ARBORETUM'S BEGINNING

The Experimental Farm system was one of early Canada's greatest national projects. Reflecting the importance of agriculture to Canada's development and prosperity, federally owned farms were created across the country in 1886 to test crops, pest control, livestock, plant material, dairy products, farm machinery, etc., and to provide results and recommendations to farmers. By 1900, about 70,000 letters from farmers seeking practical information were being answered annually by the Experimental Farms.

At the Central Experimental Farm in Ottawa, space was set aside for an Arboretum to conduct research on trees. Planting began in 1889 to test native and foreign trees and shrubs for their

Residence of the Dominion Horticulturist, W.T. Macoun.
The Macoun Memorial Garden is now at this site.
National Archives of Canada/PA-136870

Dr William Saunders

Dr James Fletcher

William T. Macoun

Arthur R. Buckley

hardiness and adaptability to the climate of the eastern Ontario and western Quebec region. Like the Farm itself, the Arboretum was laid out to create a pleasing landscape.

THE ARBORETUM'S CREATORS AND CURATORS

Dr William Saunders began what was to become much more than a successful research institution in Ottawa. A tribute to Saunders in *The Canadian Countryman* (June 20, 1936) quoted "If you would see his monument, look around," translated from an inscription on the tomb of Sir Christopher Wren. That the accolade is appropriate to a creator of the Arboretum becomes obvious to any visitor.

Prior to becoming the first Director of the Experimental Farms in 1886, Dr Saunders had been a chemist and fruit grower in London, Ontario, as well as an eminent botanist, entomologist and horticulturist. While Director, he remained an active researcher in projects that advanced farming in Canada, such as the breeding of apples that would survive the climate of western Canada.

Another man of vision who did the initial layout and planting of the Arboretum was **Dr James Fletcher**, Dominion Botanist and Entomologist. His advice to farmers and settlers with plant or insect problems was: "Just slip it in an envelope and address it to 'The Bug and Weed Man, Ottawa', never mind the stamp."

His plan was to arrange the trees in their proper botanical order. All 600 species and varieties in the Arboretum in 1893, he wrote, "are arranged to show the individual species to the greatest advantage and grouped in families. There are in nearly all cases two specimens of each kind." Dr Fletcher was in charge of the Arboretum until 1895.

W.T. Macoun took over from Fletcher and was responsible for the Arboretum until 1910. By then, the Arboretum had "one of the most extensive collections of hardy plants in America," he

Residence of the Director, Central Experimental Farm, in 1898. The William Saunders Building now occupies the site.
National Archives of Canada/PA-28041

Trevor Cole

Brian Douglas

Photo by Richard Conway

wrote. "It has been brought to its present size by a gradual but regular increase in the collection from year to year … by being constantly on the look out for new things from other institutions, botanic gardens, nurserymen and private individuals."

During that time, Macoun was in charge of thousands of other tree plantings to beautify the grounds around the buildings and lawns of the Farm. He also led research on the value of trees for timber and shelter, using forest belts planted along the northern and western boundaries of the Farm in 1887.

Macoun was described as a "man who wrote much, spoke much, and did much." He was Dominion Horticulturist until 1933, an active researcher, and worked with many organizations, both scientific and in industry.

Arthur R. Buckley was Curator of the Arboretum for thirty-five years until he retired in the early 1980s. He wrote extensively about the trees and the collection. His publication, *The Trees and Shrubs of the Dominion Arboretum*, became a valuable guide to the variety of trees and shrubs, native and cultivated, that might be planted in parks and gardens and on city streets in the Ottawa region and further afield in eastern North America, based on the results of experiments at the Arboretum.

Many others have contributed to the care and development of the Arboretum, including **H.T. Güssow**, Dominion Botanist from 1909 to 1937, **Trevor Cole**, Curator of the Arboretum after Buckley until 1994, and **Brian Douglas**, who was responsible for the Arboretum from 1994 to 2007. Each has been challenged by particular pressures and priorities and each, with their staff, has added to the value and beauty of the Arboretum.

GROWING IN THE ARBORETUM

Species from a wide range of climate zones and growing conditions are represented in the collection at the Arboretum. The Jack Pine (*Pinus banksiana*) grows on sandy dunes, the Sycamore (*Platanus occidentalis*) on flooded river valleys. The collection includes Siberian Larch (*Larix sibirica*) trees which grow in the tundra and magnolias which originate in an almost tropical habitat.

An important factor in the performance of trees in the Arboretum has been the harsh Ottawa climate. In a 2005 report, Agriculture and Agri-Food Canada (AAFC) noted that "relatively large temperature changes occur from season to season … During an average year, the normal minimum-maximum temperatures are -16°C in January and 27°C in July." (Douglas, 2005)

Many other factors have determined the current condition of the trees, from the date of their planting and the plans and priorities of Curators, to the impact of the ice storm of 1998. Although there is no longer an active science research program related to trees, many interesting new species and varieties have been planted alongside venerable old stalwarts. It continues to be an evolving collection.

DONOR TREES AND PLAQUES

Donor tree plaques are placed beside many of the trees. These plaques were installed under a joint program of the Friends of the Farm and AAFC to rejuvenate the Arboretum at a time when funding was scarce. Donors were assigned a tree and could choose to indicate on the plaque the purpose of the donation. A plaque's date refers to the date of the donation, not necessarily when the tree was planted.

Metal markers on the trees show the species name, accession number and location code. The first three digits of the accession number relate to the age of the tree. Thus, '889' for the *Pinus resinosa* in the accompanying photo, means the tree was acquired in 1889. Trees planted in the 20th century have 9 as the first digit, e.g. '926' means 1926. For the 21st century it is the first four digits that apply; thus '2002' means 2002. When the year is unknown, the first three digits are '888'.

ENVIRONMENTAL, FRUIT, ORNAMENTAL AND RESOURCE TREES

For presentation in this book, the trees are assigned to one of four categories: Environmental, Fruit, Ornamental and Resource. The category of a tree is based on its value in the local region.

A view of the Arboretum, 1895.
Dept. of Agriculture, Annual Report, 1895

Saunders, Macoun, Buckley and others may not have had these distinctions in mind when they selected the trees. As indicated in many of the texts, trees are valued for more than one reason and could properly fit in more than one category.

WHERE TO FIND THE TREES
The Arboretum is located on the east side of Prince of Wales Drive. Trees across Prince of Wales in the Campus area of the Central Experimental Farm are also included in this book. From the beginning of the Farm, trees planted around research buildings and residences, and on the open lawns in that area, have been included in tests of hardiness and ornamental value.

There are over 4,000 trees and shrubs in the Arboretum. The location of selected trees is indicated in the text. Landmarks, such as the Eastern Lookout, and area collections, such as the oaks, maples and magnolias, are indicated on the first map at the back of the book on page 236. Other maps provide suggested walks, indicating some of the trees that will be seen along the way.

CELEBRATING THE ARBORETUM AND ITS TREES
The book's photos and illustrations are of trees now living in the Arboretum. The trees may not always be the best examples of their kind; some may be close to the end of their life or before their prime, and may not always be growing in ideal conditions, but all of them are growing in the collection today.

This book is intended to celebrate a treasured collection of trees and the special, peaceful beauty of the Arboretum.

ORNAMENTAL TREES

It is hard to imagine front yards and back yards, streets and parks without trees, but that was the general situation in Canada at the time the Arboretum was established in the late 1880s. Over the years, hundreds of tree species from around the world have been tested here. Pamphlets and bulletins have been issued and advice provided about which trees were hardy in Ottawa and which showed the best ornamental qualities for the beautification of rural and urban properties and public places.

This information has helped property owners choose trees according to their particular site conditions, maintenance requirements, and aesthetic preferences. With the huge variety of common, rare, native and exotic trees now available at garden

Left: 'Leonard Messel' Magnolia
Top (left to right): Japanese Tree Lilac, Chinese Hackberry, Spruce
Above: Fraser Magnolia fruit
Right: 'Globe' Amur Corktree

Above: Koster Blue Spruce
Below: Northern Catalpa

centres in the region, it can be a great help to the shopper to see mature Ornamental trees on display throughout the year at the Arboretum.

BEAUTY ALL YEAR ROUND

Magnificent blooms appear on the magnolia trees in early spring, followed by the beautiful, fragrant flowers of the buckeyes, lilacs and catalpas. During June and July, a myriad of green hues decorate every corner of the Arboretum; light green larch shoots, shiny dark green arches on the elms, trembling white-green sycamore leaves, and dense purple-green maple foliage.

In late August and early September, more and more pinks, yellows and purples appear in the tree crowns, highlighting their diverse shapes; round, narrow, floppy or solid. These crowns then display the brilliant reds, yellows and oranges of fall. When the leaves have fallen, the solid lines of cork and ash trees contrast with the soft contours of birches and alders. On some trees, such as Japanese Tree Lilac, Kentucky Coffeetree and catalpa, the interesting seed pods are no longer hidden by the leaves. During winter months, the evergreen pine, spruce and fir trees don robes of white as their branches become laden with snow.

'Globe' Amur Corktree

Alnus hirsuta
MANCHURIAN ALDER

Simple, alternate leaves are rounded with a short point at the top.

I n the early morning a blue heron can often be seen by a grove of alder trees in the Arboretum. The trees are near the water, across from the small island. The three largest are Manchurian Alders. A.R. Buckley, former Curator of the Arboretum, described it in 1980 as "one of the best alders, and when it is growing in a suitable location it forms a handsome tree 7.5 to 9 metres high, with dark green leaves and broad pyramidal habit."

Six species of alder are native to Canada, among about 30 different species worldwide. Included in the Arboretum are the Speckled Alder (*Alnus rugosa*), or Common Alder, a shrub or small tree growing extensively across central and eastern Canada, and other alder species such as Japanese (*A. japonica*) and European White (*A. incana*).

GROWS WELL IN MOIST OR WET SITES

Like most alders, the Manchurian Alder occurs on moist or wet sites. A native of Japan, Korea, and far-east Russia, it grows in river valleys underneath large spruce, pine, and larch trees in mixed forests. It will tolerate only partial shade but will grow in poor soils. Its wood is strong, but has limited commercial value because few trees are available and the logs are small.

The Manchurian Alder is a popular ornamental tree for moist sites or water borders in cold climates. Urban developers are attracted to the tree for its ability to improve the soil, its easy cultivation and its immunity to disease and pests. While its leaves and fruits offer little nutrition to animals and birds, the Manchurian Alder provides nesting sites for small birds.

ORNAMENTAL

The Manchurian Alder is a fast growing tree with a single- or multi-stem trunk.

Bark is smooth, brown-grey with distinctive horizontal strips of glands.

Male catkins hang down. Female catkins are thicker than the male ones and grow erect. They become woody when seeds are mature and ready to disperse.

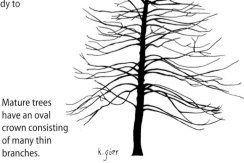

Mature trees have an oval crown consisting of many thin branches.

Fraxinus excelsior
EUROPEAN ASH

Opposite, compound leaves have a well-developed leaflet at the tip.

The tree grows more tall than wide.

h.gier

Fraxinus comes from the Greek word for hedge and this ash was often used in Europe to create hedges. European Ash populates the deciduous forests in western and eastern Europe and is one of the tallest trees on European plains. It grows in very rich, moist soils with oaks, elms and lindens.

STATUESQUE WITH GRACEFUL LEAVES

A.R. Buckley, former Curator of the Arboretum, described the leaves of the European Ash as being "more graceful" than those of the White Ash, although not as colourful in the fall. European Ash trees grow alongside Red and White Ash at the southern end of the Arboretum and in the northern area near the poplars. In 2005, there were also five ornamental cultivars growing around the Arboretum.

European Ash trees are often planted as ornamental specimens in parks and green spaces. Young ones grow well in partial shade but full sun is needed for mature trees. They are tolerant of urban pollution, fast growing, and liable to spread.

PRIZED FOR ITS WOOD

The wood of the European Ash has strength and elasticity; welcome qualities in furniture-making and construction.

In winter, deer and small rodents eat twigs of the European Ash, whose seeds provide food for squirrels and mice. This tree is not threatened by dangerous diseases or pests in the Arboretum although borers can damage the trunk and make it susceptible to other infestations.

ORNAMENTAL

The European Ash reaches maturity in less than 50 years, but growth continues for hundreds of years. On solitary trees, the crowns are very long.

Its light grey bark has irregular corky plates divided by narrow furrows.

Long, winged seeds hang on trees through the winter and remain dormant several years after dispersal.

Dense clusters of male (left) and loose panicles of female (right) flowers appear before the leaves and can occur on the same or different trees. (The female flowers are those of European Ash 'Globosa'.) Twigs are thick and have prominent black buds, which are especially noticeable in winter.

Betula nigra

RIVER BIRCH

The River Birch species was first planted in the Arboretum in 1893. A graceful young River Birch specimen stands beside the bridge to the small island. It displays the broad outline, the flaky and curling bark and the large leaves, which led A.R. Buckley, former Curator of the Arboretum, to describe it in 1980 as "one of the most interesting trees in the Arboretum."

River Birch trees thrive under water-soaked conditions although they do not survive prolonged floods. They grow along the banks of the Mississippi and other rivers and streams in the south-eastern part of the United States. Along with Sycamore, Silver Maple, honey locust and others, the River Birch colonizes open spaces on moist, alluvial soils after forest disturbances.

Alternate, simple leaves are dark green with toothed edges. They turn bright yellow in the fall.

GOOD ORNAMENTAL VALUE

Although the quality of its wood is poor, the wood colour and texture, as well as the ornamental and environmental qualities of the River Birch, make it a popular tree. It has been planted in city parks and on reclamation sites far beyond its natural range.

River Birch provides good shelter and nesting sites for many birds, which feed in winter on immature male catkins. Deer munch on the twigs and leaves of young trees. This birch does not face dangerous diseases and pests, and is resistant to Bronze Birch Borer which destroys other birches.

Hanging-down male catkins appear on tips of twigs in fall and open in the spring. Upright female catkins emerge on thin branches in early spring.

Mature seeds are dispersed in early summer.

Twigs are thin and grow upright.

River Birch trees are fast growing but, like other birch species, do not live long. In sunny locations, trees can become large with wide irregular crowns. On medium size trunks and big branches, the bark has curly, papery plates in a variety of colours.

Catalpa ovata

CHINESE CATALPA

The creamy yellow flowers of the Chinese Catalpa are smaller than those of the Northern Catalpa, but the leaves are as large and conspicuous, making this another striking specimen in the Arboretum. The largest among them are found beside the southern path as it curls eastward past the oaks and butternuts.

HARDY THROUGHOUT THE ARBORETUM

Other species of catalpa were tested in the early years of the Arboretum but, according to A.R. Buckley, former Curator of the Arboretum, the Chinese Catalpa was "the only catalpa tried in the Arboretum that can be considered absolutely hardy in whatever location it is planted."

Chinese Catalpa originated on mountain slopes in mixed forests of north-eastern China. There it grew with oaks, Korean Pines, birches and others. It tolerates poor and dry sites, but needs open space and fertile soils for the best growth.

SHOWY BLOSSOMS AND LARGE LEAVES ARE GOOD FOR CITIES AND PARKS

The tree was introduced to North American cities and parks because of its showy blossoms and large attractive leaves. It is resistant to city pollution, but disease can turn its leaves brown in midsummer. Catalpa wood is brittle. Heavy snow, ice, or strong winds can snap branches.

The flowers are very attractive to bees and other pollinators, and small birds hide their nests inside the dense crown.

Pale yellow or whitish flowers have both stamens and pistils.

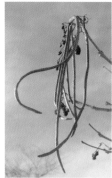

After pollination, the flowers produce long, cylindrical pods with hairy seeds inside. These pods stay on the tree during winter.

Bark is thin with some loose strips on old trees.

The Chinese Catalpa grows quickly, but never becomes a large tree.

Opposite leaves are hairless underneath, unlike those of the Northern Catalpa.

The crowns of mature trees are irregular.

Catalpa speciosa
NORTHERN CATALPA

A group of Northern Catalpa is found on the Southern Walk east of the hawthorns near the water. Introduced to eastern Ontario from the Mississippi Valley in the United States, the Northern Catalpa likes wet forests and river banks.

A "SHOWY" TREE

Because of its beauty, rapid growth, and tolerance of urban conditions, it is widely used in landscaping. W.T. Macoun, writing in 1925 about the trees of the Arboretum, said this was "…a very striking-looking tree of rapid growth, and the large, showy, white-and-purple flowers… are a fine sight. The very large leaves also help this tree give a semi-tropical effect to the landscape." The Northern Catalpa takes just 15 to 20 years to mature.

Clusters of bell-shaped flowers, white with yellow stripes and purple spots, appear in June.

KNOWN AS BEAN-TREES

With seed pods that resemble runner beans, Catalpas are also known as Bean-trees. Other names for this tree are Western Catalpa, Catawba and Cigar Tree. The seed pods are of little value to wildlife. Insects pollinate the beautiful flowers when searching for sweet syrup.

Mildew and twig blight can sometimes affect the appearance of the tree in late summer.

Broad, smooth leaves are light green on top, paler underneath.

ORNAMENTAL

Long, conspicuous seed pods mature in the fall and hang open on the tree throughout the winter.

It is a small tree about 10-15 m high with a dense, oval crown when mature.

fyi Speciosa *means "showy" or "beautiful".*

Bark is greyish-brown with shallow furrows.

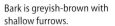

k. gier

Thuja standishii
JAPANESE ARBORVITAE

"The Japanese Arborvitae is a splendid small tree … It is much more of the spreading type than the native arborvitae, having one to four distinct trunks and a broad pyramidal outline … The leaves make it stand out in the Arboretum in winter because they remain green all the time, whereas other arborvitae leaves change to a dull brown."

A.R. BUCKLEY, FORMER CURATOR OF THE ARBORETUM

As the name suggests, the Japanese Arborvitae originates in Japan, in conifer forests on high mountains. It is one of the "Five Sacred Trees of Kiso" often used for Shinto temple construction. It grows alongside fir, pine, yew and hemlock trees, but only in moist soils. Its wood is knotty, soft and resistant to decay. The species was introduced in 1860 from seeds supplied to the Standish Nursery in England; hence the name.

Twigs and shoots are flat with scaly leaves.

As ornamental evergreens, Japanese Arborvitae have uses in landscaping similar to Eastern White Cedars, but they are rare in North America. In urban environments and parks, Japanese Arborvitae trees do not attract serious pests or diseases. Specimens can live in parks for over two hundred years. There is only one mature Japanese Arborvitae now in the Arboretum, at the north end, down the slope from Building 72.

fyi *Japanese Arborvitae leaves are generally dark green, top and bottom, as compared with those of Eastern White Cedar which are a lighter green on the bottom.*

ARBORVITAE OR CEDAR?

Arborvitae means "tree of life," a term originating in the mid 16th century. In 1535, the crew of Jacques Cartier's exploring expedition to Canada avoided scurvy by drinking tea brewed from the leaves of an evergreen tree. It is not known which species it was. "*Arbor vitae*" seeds were taken to France by Cartier and planted in the King's gardens at Fontainebleau.

The genus *Thuja* is commonly known as cedar, as well as arborvitae. Thus, *Thuja occidentalis* is called both Eastern White Cedar and Eastern Arborvitae. Cedar, however, refers to *Cedrus*, an entirely different family of trees, such as the famed cedars of Lebanon. *Thuja* is the Latin name for an aromatic tree.

Male and female cones are solitary and grow on the same tree. Ripe female cones open in the fall and disperse small, two-winged seeds.

The thin bark is reddish in colour and forms long, narrow strips on large trunks.

Large limbs often curve outwards at the base of the crown, making it very wide.

k.gier

A Japanese Arborvitae tree is slow growing and long living, with a dense crown.

Aesculus
BUCKEYES AND HORSE CHESTNUTS

Red Horse Chestnut *(Aesculus × carnea)*

Baumann Horse Chestnut
(Aesculus hippocastanum)

Bottlebrush Buckeye
(Aesculus parviflora)

The *Aesculus* genus includes about 23 species. Those originating in North America are usually called buckeyes while those from other continents are called horse chestnuts. The Horse Chestnut (*Aesculus hippocastanum*) itself, for example, comes from Europe.

The split seed-capsule of the buckeye is thought to resemble the half-opened eye of a deer. Pioneers in Ohio called themselves Buckeyes and the Ohio Buckeye is the official state tree.

A good representation of buckeyes and horse chestnuts, both large and small, is present in the Arboretum. Among the excellent large specimens in the maple area are Ohio Buckeye, Painted Buckeye and Yellow Buckeye. Striking, large Baumann Horse Chestnut trees grace the open Campus area across Prince of Wales Driveway.

Also in the maple area is a Bottlebrush Buckeye (*A. parviflora*). This plant, from the southern United States, is very tender and most unusual in Ottawa. Always a shrub, its flowers open when all its leaves are completely developed, much later than other buckeyes. With its "glorious spikes of bloom in July," it was described in 1980 by A.R. Buckley, former Curator of the Arboretum, as "one of the most beautiful of all large shrubs in the Arboretum."

Another small variety, the Red Horse Chestnut (*A. × carnea*), was first planted in the Arboretum in 1893. This tree is very showy, with its red-yellow flowers.

Buckeyes and horse chestnuts have poisonous nuts and roots. They can also create a messy area underfoot when the nuts fall. Nevertheless, when in full leaf and flower, they are lovely ornamental trees.

Aesculus glabra
OHIO BUCKEYE

"This has made a fine attractive-looking tree at Ottawa, and has reached a height of about 40 feet. While the flowers are not as ornamental as the Horse Chestnut, it is much hardier, the leaves are healthier, it fruits abundantly, and is altogether a desirable small ornamental tree."

A spiky husk covers one or two nuts and opens by splitting into three segments.

This was how W. T. Macoun, former Dominion Horticulturist, described the Ohio Buckeye in 1925. First planted in the Arboretum in 1893, the oldest Ohio Buckeye can be seen in the maple section. The spiky husks on the nuts distinguish it from the smooth husks of the other buckeye species in the area. The Ohio Buckeye tends to flower a little earlier than the others.

THE ONLY *AESCULUS* NATIVE TO CANADA

The Ohio Buckeye is native to those central North American deciduous forests which cover the bottomlands of river valleys. First noted in 1982 in southwestern Ontario, it is Canada's only indigenous *Aesculus* species. In old growth forests, it accompanies Bur Oak, White Ash, Black Walnut and other large trees. Deep, fertile and moist soils are preferred by this tree, which never grows on depleted sites. Young trees are able to tolerate shade for many years.

The wood of the Ohio Buckeye is soft and weak, and has few uses for manufacture. The nuts are also of little value but thick foliage and many flowers make this a good tree for landscapers. The dense crown of the Ohio Buckeye attracts nesting birds, though the nuts and leaves are inedible for some animals. Frost, pests and diseases can do some damage to these trees and their most dangerous threats in urban environments are air pollution and wounds on their trunks or limbs caused by rot and fungi.

Opposite leaves consist of 5 leaflets attached to a long stalk. They release an unpleasant odour when crushed, as do other parts of the tree when bruised: hence, another common name for the tree is Fetid Buckeye.

An Ohio Buckeye tree grows slowly, taking decades to develop a dense, oval crown.

Flowers grow in big upright clusters. Lower flowers have stamens and pistils; upper ones have only stamens.

The bark is rough, scaly, and relatively thin.

Twigs are thick with big, sharp-pointed, non-sticky buds on their tips and prominent horseshoe-shaped leaf scars.

The branches are arching, often descending to the ground.

k.gier

Aesculus hippocastanum
HORSE CHESTNUT

Large leaves (top) with seven leaflets create dense shade. Big, upright clusters of white flowers (above) appear when leaves are fully developed. The bottom flowers in each cluster are female.

The Horse Chestnut originated in Europe where its natural range is now confined to ravines and creek valleys in the Balkan Mountains. A relic of prehistoric forests, it grows with hornbeam, walnut, ash, and other deciduous Mediterranean trees. The largest trees grow on moist sites with deep, fertile soils. Its scarce wood is soft and not at all durable.

Very ornamental when in full leaf and flower, the Horse Chestnut is widely planted where there is space in parks and on large lawns in Europe and North America. It was also naturalized in forest plantations on the east coast of North America.

Horse Chestnut trees are not victims of dangerous pests and diseases in North America and, given enough space to grow, they will tolerate urban environments. While their leaves and nuts are inedible to humans and some wildlife, the flowers are good nectar producers, attracting bees and other pollinators.

NOT QUITE HARDY ENOUGH FOR THE ARBORETUM

First planted in the Arboretum in 1890, the Horse Chestnut has not proved to be reliably hardy, but can survive in sheltered places.

Two young Horse Chestnut trees, planted by Brian Douglas, Foreman of the Arboretum and Ornamental Gardens, are growing in the nut collection at the south end and in the maple area. The only mature Horse Chestnut trees, as in the photos and drawing, are Baumann Horse Chestnuts (*Aesculus hippocastanum* 'Baumannii') in the Campus area of the Farm between Birch Drive and Prince of Wales Driveway. This hardy variety has long-lasting, double flowers that do not produce nuts, so it is less messy.

The Horse Chestnut is a massive tree with a vast, rounded crown and large trunk.

Large, sticky buds are prominent on ends of stout twigs.

Bark is thin, but coarse on old trees.

The female flowers produce large, rounded nuts encased in spiky husks, which split to release the nuts, also known as 'conkers'.

Numerous thick branches and twigs give a coarse appearance to the tree during winter.

k.gier

Aesculus sylvatica
PAINTED BUCKEYE

Irregular flowers have stamens and pistils. They grow in long (10-15 cm), upright clusters and vary in colour from yellow-green to orange-yellow.

Opposite-growing leaves consist of five leaflets which are pale green underneath.

The large, showy flowers of the Painted Buckeye vary in colour, suggesting the work of an artist's paint brush. This feature and its attractive leaves which cast a dense shade, have made this ornamental tree popular with urban landscapers. Mature specimens can be found in the maple section of the Arboretum, along with other buckeye species.

The Painted Buckeye was discovered more than two centuries ago by William Bartram, an early American botanist. It is also known as Georgia Buckeye, growing naturally underneath tall oak, beech, or hickory trees in the deciduous forests of mid-eastern North America. On either low mountain slopes or plains, the Painted Buckeye prefers rich and moist soil. The Latin species name *sylvatica* means "of the woods".

ALSO KNOWN AS DWARF BUCKEYE
Painted Buckeyes never grow into big trees and are sometimes just shrubs. Another name for the species is Dwarf Buckeye. The small size does not appeal to loggers, who find few uses for the wood.

Only the flowers of Painted Buckeyes are acceptable food for some birds, the nuts being bitter and inedible, except for squirrels. Cultivated trees are free of pests and diseases. When there is no heavy pollution or soil compaction, the species will do well in cities. Apart from the chore of cleaning up fallen nuts, the trees are easy to maintain.

Painted Buckeye forms a rounded, dense crown even in shady places.

k. sier

Painted Buckeye is a small tree or multi-stemmed shrub.

Relatively thick twigs often have two big, non-resinous buds at the end.

Thin bark is grey or light brown. Smooth when young, it becomes scaly with age.

Flowers produce a single nut or a cluster (left). Each is covered by a smooth husk which splits into three segments when the fruit is mature.

The husks (right) open on the tree in late summer and release dark brown nuts. This differs from walnut trees, whose husks fall to the ground with the nuts.

Aesculus flava
YELLOW BUCKEYE

This is the largest of the buckeyes, often planted where a showy specimen tree is needed in a landscape. The flowers of the mature Yellow Buckeye in the maple area of the Arboretum may not be as individually attractive as those of the other buckeyes nearby, but the effect of the flowers and foliage in the long, high crown of the tree is particularly striking.

Opposite leaves with five leaflets become yellow-orange in the fall.

CASTS A DENSE SHADE

A.R. Buckley, former Curator of the Arboretum, remarked on the dense shade thrown by the leaves of the Yellow Buckeye. Another name for it is Sweet Buckeye and distinctive features are the large scales that cover the bark when it ages.

Yellow Buckeye is native to eastern regions of North America. It grows with oaks, maples, and ash trees on moist and fertile soils along river valleys and stream banks. Occurring in old forests, the species is not able to grow in recently logged areas or on nutrient depleted sites.

A FEATURE IN AN ORNAMENTAL LANDSCAPE

Though the wood of Yellow Buckeyes is soft, with little commercial value in the lumber industry, the real value of these trees is ornamental. They are much appreciated by landscape architects who have found many uses for their freestanding decorative features.

One to three round nuts are enclosed in a smooth husk. Such husks become noticeable on trees in mid summer.

The extensive crown of the Yellow Buckeye provides good shelter for nesting birds, but the fruit and foliage of the tree is inedible for animals and birds. This buckeye is less susceptible to diseases and pests than others, but leaf scorch and blotch may be a problem. Rotten stems and branches may be a hazard for utility lines or nearby buildings.

fyi *A Yellow Buckeye grows slowly, reaching over 20 m in height.*

Topmost buds are big and smooth.

The bark on this old tree is thin with shallow, corky scales. On young trees, the bark is smooth and thin.

The crown is lengthy with big upright branches. This tree in the Arboretum is crowded by its neighbours. Elsewhere, if the tree is exposed to the sun, the branches will start at the bottom of the trunk.

Individual flowers are bisexual at the top of panicles. Only male flowers grow at the base.

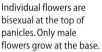

Gymnocladus dioicus
KENTUCKY COFFEETREE

W ith the largest leaves of any native tree in Canada and its dangling pods, the Kentucky Coffeetree has an exotic, southern look.

Because it is late to show leaves in the spring and early to lose them, this tree was given the Greek name *Gymnocladus*, meaning "naked branch." The species was first planted in the Arboretum in 1890 and a fine old tree stands at the entrance to the Arboretum at Prince of Wales Drive. Younger trees are beside it and another young one can be found at the northern end of the Arboretum among the Black Walnuts and Butternuts. Other trees can be found in the Campus area.

NATIVE TO CANADA, BUT RARE
Although a native tree, the Kentucky Coffeetree is only rarely found in southwestern Ontario and is also uncommon throughout the deciduous forests of central North America. Scattered individual trees grow in ravines and on lower slopes where honey locust, hackberry, and poplars re-colonize forest lands. Sunny, moist sites with deep soils are the best for this tree, but it easily survives periodic droughts.

Cabinetmakers value Kentucky Coffeetree wood which is hard, with a fine texture. Kentucky Coffeetrees rarely adorn towns and cities despite their tolerance of drought, salt spray, and air pollution.

THE PIONEERS' COFFEE SUBSTITUTE
Early settlers roasted the seeds as a coffee substitute, hence the popular name for the tree. Raw seeds are poisonous to humans, and animals find the twigs, leaves and fruits of the tree inedible. It does not have serious diseases or pests, and is easy to grow from seed.

Leaves are massive and complex. They are double compound, with alternately-arranged leaflets. The huge leaves cast dense shade, despite a lack of numerous small branches.

An oval-shaped crown consists of many upright branches showing an obvious zigzag pattern.

k.gier

Bark of a mature tree is rough, with thick, scaly ridges.

Twigs are stout with large leaf scars.

Fleshy pods remain on a tree long after leaf-fall.

The Kentucky Coffeetree is slow growing and does not become very large.

Flowers (left) that are male, female, or bisexual may grow on the same tree or on different trees. They gather in loose clusters on top of new shoots.

Phellodendron amurense

AMUR CORKTREE

The Amur Corktree was named for its corky bark. The genus name comes from the Greek words *phellos* (cork) and *dendron* (tree). In fact, the bark is not thick enough to produce cork, which comes from an unrelated species, the Cork Oak (*Quercus suber*).

A HAVEN FOR SHADE LOVERS

Large Amur Corktrees provide shade south of the magnolia collection, near the giant Wych Elm. Other mature corktrees on top of the slope across the path from the maples are especially picturesque in fall and winter with their berries and bare branches framed against the sky. The corktree in the photo (opposite) is in the Ornamental Gardens, where there is also a beautiful 'Globe' Amur Corktree, with the same attractive bark, wide-spreading branches and black berries.

Amur Corktrees occur naturally in mixed forests in China, Korea and Japan on moist mountain slopes, flood plains and the banks of streams. They tolerate various soils but prefer fertile soils, avoiding poor, sandy sites. Although the tree is pest-free in urban environments, it may suffer from city pollutants. The species may spread due to seed dispersal by birds, but it will not colonize poor sites.

The heavy, hard wood of this tree is used in cabinet-making and for specific products like gun stocks. The Amur Corktree attracts numerous nectar-hunting insects and birds. Its leaves and fruit are also palatable for animals and birds.

Opposite, compound leaves (top) consist of uneven numbers of dark green leaflets; fragrant when crushed, turning yellow in the fall.

Berry-like black fruits (above) with black seeds may remain on female trees throughout the winter (right).

fyi *Amur Corktree is a long living tree, strong and healthy to over 100 years of age.*

Horseshoe-shaped leaf scars, embracing small buds, are seen on thick twigs.

Furrowed, grey bark is thick, soft and elastic to the touch.

Female and male flowers in terminal upright clusters occur separately on different trees. Flowers are small, but rich in nectar.

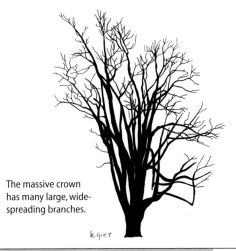

The massive crown has many large, wide-spreading branches.

k.gier

Taxodium distichum
BALD CYPRESS

Alternate small shoots with two rows of soft needles emerge in the spring and they fall off in the autumn.

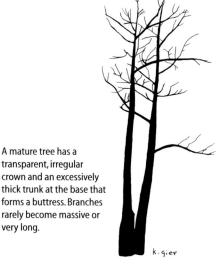

A mature tree has a transparent, irregular crown and an excessively thick trunk at the base that forms a buttress. Branches rarely become massive or very long.

k.gier

One expects to see Bald Cypress trees in the swamps of southeastern U.S., not in Ottawa, and yet they have been in the Arboretum since 1893. After six years from that first planting, the species was rated as "half hardy," meaning that an average winter would kill back a quarter to one half of new growth. Just one mature tree is in the Arboretum now, in the maple area next to Prince of Wales Drive, but there are young ones to watch, planted by Brian Douglas, Foreman of the Arboretum and Ornamental Gardens.

EXQUISITE FEATHERY FOLIAGE

Like the larch, the Bald Cypress is a conifer that sheds its needle-like leaves in the fall. "Their exquisite feathery foliage, which turns golden in the fall before it drops to the ground, is ornamental," wrote A.R. Buckley, former Curator of the Arboretum, in 1980. It is "bald" because it loses not only its leaves in winter but also its twigs. The Latin name *distichum* means "two rows," referring to the way the leaves grow.

Also known as Swamp Cypress, the Bald Cypress is native to the Atlantic and Mexican Gulf coastal areas of the U.S., where it can live more than a thousand years. It grows in swamps and wetlands together with magnolia, oak, ash and maple trees. Nutrient rich and oversaturated soils are preferred, but in cultivation it tolerates dry upland sites with less fertile soils.

NO SEEDS IN OTTAWA

Cold weather limits cultivation of the Bald Cypress outside its natural range. Ottawa's environment is far from ideal for this tree. The specimens in the Arboretum have not been known to produce seeds. Nevertheless, with its soft, feathery foliage, it is a fine ornamental for a large space.

ORNAMENTAL

Bark is thin with an
interwoven pattern.

The wood of the Bald Cypress resists decay and was widely used by shipbuilders and for docks. Bald Cypress trees sustain many wildlife species. Ospreys and bald eagles use large trees for nesting and breeding. The tree does not have critical pests or diseases.

fyi *In its natural habitat, Bald Cypress is a large, slow-growing and durable tree. In colder areas, as in the Arboretum, growth is limited and lifespan is short.*

Ulmus glabra
WYCH ELM

fyi *Wych is pronounced "witch".*

Leaves have an asymmetric base and distinctive forks in the veins at the ends.

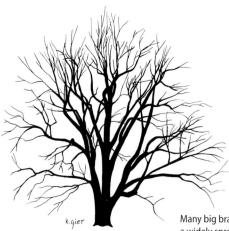

k.gier

Many big branches support a widely spread crown.

A n impressive old Wych Elm grows at the northern end of the Arboretum next to the magnolia collection. Its stately structure and umbrella shape make it a perfect subject for visiting artists who come to capture the beauty of the Arboretum on canvas.

URBAN BEAUTIES, NOW SCARCE

These large trees, also known as Scotch Elms, originated in Europe and Asia in mixed forests of oak, maple, linden and ash. In North America, they are found at forest edges and in urban settings. Unfortunately, numerous insect and fungal problems are associated with the Wych Elm. The most serious is the fatal Dutch Elm Disease, which has destroyed the elm population in many cities. The species is also susceptible to many urban pollutants.

Elms were well represented in the early days of the Arboretum. In 1904, 92 species and varieties of elm were reported to have been doing well there. The National Capital Commission Driveway through the Farm was formerly called Elm Avenue, with a tunnel-like canopy of drooping elms.

Elms continue to grace the Arboretum, including magnificent older specimens such as the Wych Elm pictured here. An enchanting path at the east side is lined with young American Elms and hackberries. *The Living Collection of the Dominion Arboretum* (Douglas, 2005) lists 22 species and varieties.

ORNAMENTAL

This species grows in parks, along roadsides and in urban green spaces, where trees can live for 100 years or more.

Bark is a furrowed grey and is smoother than that of other elms.

Seeds are contained in wafer-like samaras.

Ulmus pumila

SIBERIAN ELM

Alternate leaves are about 5 cm long, glossy, dark green and, unlike other elms, have an almost symmetrical base.

fyi Pumila *is Latin for dwarf or small.*

Siberian Elm has a globular crown with many large limbs growing on a short trunk. Twigs, which often hang down, are slender and easy to break.

k·gier

Ottawa as "a city without elms" was foreseen by Arthur Buckley, former Curator of the Arboretum, because of the ravages of disease affecting the trees. Fortunately, this dire prediction has not come true. The species that is perhaps the most resistant to Dutch Elm Disease is the Siberian Elm. Its tolerance of poor soils, summer droughts and cold winters, have made it a desirable tree for site rehabilitation throughout North America.

SMALL AND GRACEFUL

The Siberian Elm is also ornamental. W.T. Macoun, former Dominion Horticulturist, included the Siberian Elm in his 1925 list of best ornamental deciduous trees that had proven to be hardy at Ottawa. He wrote, "This is a rapid-growing small tree with small leaves, and makes a rather graceful specimen. Where there is room for small trees other than those with conspicuous flowers, this elm might be planted with good effect."

A few trees of this species and an old specimen of the 'Dropmore' cultivar can be found at the northern end of the Arboretum, close to Prince of Wales Drive.

ORIGINATES IN ASIA AND RUSSIA

The Siberian Elm came from the sparse forests covering dry slopes in northern China, Korea and the far east of Russia. Since its introduction in the mid 19th century, the species has been planted in parks, urban green spaces and on farmlands. Its wood is brittle with little commercial value.

Small rodents and birds may consume the abundant seed crop in early summer. Numerous insect and fungal problems are associated

Siberian Elm is a fast growing tree with a wide spreading crown. It is smaller than the Wych Elm.

Early in spring, clusters of tiny, pale green flowers appear on most thin branches.

Bark is grey and becomes deeply furrowed on mature trees.

with the species, but nothing is critical. Well established trees produce sprouts and suckers which are difficult to control. As a result, despite its resistance to Dutch Elm Disease and street pollutants, the Siberian Elm is used with caution by landscapers.

Mature fruits are greenish, wafer-like samaras 1 to 2 cm in diameter. Seeds do not have a dormancy period and germinate when fallen to the ground in early summer.

Pseudotsuga menziesii
DOUGLAS-FIR

"The Douglas-fir is a very majestic and handsome tree, with foliage dark green above and silvery beneath." W.T. MACOUN, FORMER DOMINION HORTICULTURIST, 1897

Sharp pointed buds and lemon-smelling needles (when crushed) distinguish the Douglas-fir from true fir trees, which have similar twigs.

Seed cones develop distinctive three-pointed bracts. Mature cones release their seeds in the fall and remain seedless on the tree through the winter.

The oldest Douglas-fir is near the entrance to the Arboretum in the Circle area. Planted in 1889, it is one of the oldest trees in the collection and has acquired a unique shape with a slight lean. Stately specimens of Douglas-fir can be seen elsewhere in the Arboretum and in the Campus area. The Douglas-fir also proved to be among the best tall evergreen hedges in the experimental hedge collection. Planted in 1894, the Douglas-fir hedge can still be seen close to Maple Drive.

The Latin name means false hemlock and, indeed, the species is unrelated to hemlock. Neither is it a fir tree, as the common name suggests. One difference is that the cones hang down on the Douglas-fir rather than being erect, as are the cones on firs. The common name refers to David Douglas, the Scottish botanical explorer of North America in the 1820s. The name *menziesii* honours Archibald Menzies, Scottish botanist on George Vancouver's voyage of exploration along the Pacific coast of North America in 1792.

A MOST VALUABLE WOOD

Douglas-fir trees grow in the mountains from central British Columbia to Mexico. The trees form dense, dark forests along with fir and spruce on moist ridges in Canada.

Douglas-fir lumber, which is long, strong and durable, is among the most valued woods on the market and is used in all types of construction. Seeds of Douglas-fir trees support populations of small birds and animals. Twig blight and aphids can destroy the needles, but more serious problems do not occur in the Arboretum.

This old Douglas-fir (left) is near the entrance to the Arboretum.

Douglas-fir trees grow fast, becoming tall and massive, and survive for centuries on favourable sites. A long conical crown consists of almost horizontal, thin branches.

Bark is very thick and coarse on large, mature trees.

Pollen-bearing cones (far left) hang down and young female cones (left) grow upright on the same branch.

Abies cephalonica
GREEK FIR

A handsome Greek Fir with a perfect conical shape stands in the Circle near the Southern Lookout. In the Arboretum in 1899, this species was rated as "half hardy," meaning that a quarter to a half of new growth would tend to be killed back in winter. Nevertheless, this particular tree has survived many hard winters.

DENSE TO THE GROUND

The thick, densely set branches and leaves, features of the Greek Fir, reach right to the ground. Unique among firs in the Ottawa region, according to A.R. Buckley, former Curator of the Arboretum, are the "sharp prickles" at the tips of its needles.

Greek Fir originates in the Mediterranean, but is now rare in that region, occurring naturally on high mountain slopes in the Balkans. It grows on moist to dry sites in mixed forests, together with pine, spruce, beech, and juniper trees. It tolerates a variety of soils, but not heavy clays. It was widely sought by lumbermen in the past for its long, straight trunks and light, soft wood, used for the masts of ships and in the construction of Greek and Roman houses. It is often planted in parks and big gardens in Europe and less frequently in North America. This species is disappearing from natural forests.

Greek Fir, like other firs, has seeds and buds that are edible for birds and rodents. When growing out of its natural range it is not affected by dangerous pests or diseases, but its cultivation is limited by cold climate and urban pollutants.

Male and female cones appear on the same tree.

After pollination, upright female cones are prominent features on top branches. Mature cones disintegrate and release winged seeds in the fall.

If a Greek Fir tree grows in a sunny spot, like this one in the Arboretum, it will become tall and massive in a few decades with long, lower branches close to the ground. The crown is dense with many horizontal twigs and branches on which needles remain for up to 7 years.

Bark is thin on both young and mature trees. Older trees develop scales on the outer surface.

Individual needles are flat and grow in spirals on twigs, similar to those on spruce trees.

Celtis sinensis

CHINESE HACKBERRY

Alternate leaves are glossy green and turn yellow in fall. As with the Common Hackberry, flowers are tiny, appearing in spring at the same time as shoots and leaves.

Small reddish-orange berries persist on the Chinese Hackberry until late fall.

An old Chinese Hackberry stands atop the slope running down to Dow's Lake near the Eastern Lookout, with other hackberries as close neighbours. It has not always proved to be hardy in the Arboretum. A.R. Buckley, former Curator of the Arboretum, reported in 1980 that six Chinese Hackberry trees had all succumbed to the winter.

FROM CHINA'S COOL DECIDUOUS FORESTS

The Chinese Hackberry is one of the species in the cool-temperate deciduous forests of China, Korea and Japan. The hackberry tree, up to 20 m high, occurs in large numbers in dry oak-dominated woodlands at low elevations. It grows on clayish and sandy soils, and does not survive on sites with stagnant water.

The hard, breakable wood of this tree is sold on local markets primarily as firewood. Landscape architects have few uses for the Chinese Hackberry in North America, although, being pollution and drought resistant, it is a very good tree for lining streets, and dry sites.

k.gier

It develops a vast crown with few big limbs and many thin branches.

fyi The Chinese Hackberry grows quickly and casts good shade.

PEST AND DISEASE FREE

The Chinese Hackberry's edible berries attract birds and small rodents which help disperse the hard-shelled seeds. Heart rot can decompose the inner parts of old trunks or limbs but otherwise this tree is free of pests and disease.

On large trunks and branches, the bark is corky and coarse.

Crataegus
HAWTHORNS

These clusters of perfect, white flowers and glossy, leathery leaves were seen on a Dotted Hawthorn (*Crataegus punctata*) in the Circle area.

Bright red Hawthorn berries become very attractive in mid summer.

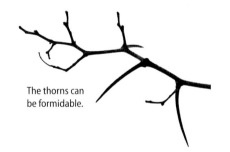

The thorns can be formidable.

Diversity among Hawthorn trees is impressive as seen in many beautiful trees and shrubs in the hawthorn area, in the poplar area and elsewhere in the Arboretum.

Hawthorns were first planted in the Arboretum in the 1890s. By 1904, the collection included 116 different species and varieties. About ten trees have survived from the original plantings. In 2005, 47 species and varieties were listed in *The Living Collection of the Dominion Arboretum* (Douglas, 2005).

In spring, many of the trees have attractive white flowers, which form a pleasing contrast with dark green, glossy leaves of various shapes, deeply lobed, toothed or smooth. Hawthorn fruit, also known as haws and hawberries, are like small apples, edible and tasty. They can be difficult to collect because of sharp thorns. Another common name for the tree is Thornapple. Because of their thorns, Hawthorns have been commonly used as boundary markers and protective hedges. Some examples can be seen among the hedgerows in the Ornamental Gardens.

The bark is thin and scaly. Relatively small trunks, often multi-stemmed and of irregular shape, provide shelter for birds and small animals.

"Among the interesting things planted this year may be mentioned a fine collection of *Crataegus* donated by the Arnold Arboretum," wrote W.T. Macoun in 1905. A specimen from that time is shown above and below.

k.giet

Hawthorn trees can be ornamental in spring, summer and fall; in winter, as well, if the birds leave the fruit alone.

fyi *It is very difficult to tell Hawthorn species apart. Experts disagree on whether to classify them as shrubs or trees, and on the number of species. Claims range from fewer than a hundred to more than a thousand.*

Cercidiphyllum japonicum

KATSURA TREE

I n 1896, W.T. Macoun, former Dominion Horticulturist, described the Katsura Tree as "very striking." He liked its rather small, heart-shaped leaves which "give the tree a very light appearance." The tree has a broad, pyramid shape with many branches, but is compact. In 1980, A.R. Buckley suggested it was "One of the best trees for small home gardens."

A FAVOURITE FOR LANDSCAPING

Since the late 19th century, landscape architects in North America have been planting this tree in parks, on golf courses and along residential streets. A Katsura Tree dating from 1947 can be seen in the Arboretum on the south side of the magnolia collection. A younger one, about twenty years old, is nearby.

Katsura Trees occur naturally in the cool, temperate forests of eastern Asia. They grow among huge beech, lime, walnut, and horse chestnut trees on mountain slopes. These natural habitats are humid, and Katsura Trees in cultivation are sensitive to any lack of water. The soft and fine grained wood of this species is known on Asian and North American markets, but it is rare and expensive.

Insects, birds and animals are not attracted to Katsura Tree pollen, leaves or seeds. The dense foliage, however, provides good protection for nests. The tree does not face any significant risk of disease or pests in North America. On moist and fertile sites, a Katsura Tree is easy to grow, and only its big, shallow roots can cause problems for lawn mowers and paved surfaces.

Simple leaves turn bright orange-yellow in the fall.

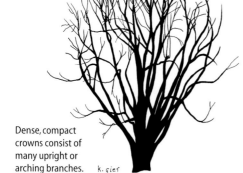

Dense, compact crowns consist of many upright or arching branches. k. çier

ORNAMENTAL

Katsura Trees grow quickly when young. Mature trees are single- or multi-stemmed.

Twigs are long and have many pairs of buds on short branchlets.

The bark is thin with shallow furrows and, on old trunks, can form loose plates.

Male and female flowers grow on separate trees and appear at the same time as leaves. Later in the summer, small pods with many winged seeds can be seen on female trees.

Larix
LARCHES

"What could be more beautiful than the Larch in spring with its long necklaces of soft green shoots hanging from the branches and the pink, green, or rose-tinted cones? What can equal the brilliant golden effect of Larch leaves in fall and the entrancing beauty of its twigs during winter?"

The Larches in the Arboretum continue to be a surprise and delight, as they were for A.R. Buckley, former Curator of the Arboretum, when he wrote the foregoing in 1965. They have beauty in summer as well, with the appeal of an evergreen and yet with a soft, open texture which gives only a light shade, making it easy to keep the grass growing underneath.

Larches are conifers, not evergreens. They shed their needles each fall. Most of the ten species in the world are represented in the Arboretum and were among the earliest trees planted there.

The wood of all Larches is durable and very heavy; so heavy that logs do not float, which ruled out transportation by river flotation. Uses of the wood have included railroad ties, telephone poles, bridges and boat timbers.

All Larch species are similar in detail, which makes it difficult to distinguish species by comparing twigs, needles and cones. Differences between Larches are easier to spot from a distance, with each species having unique crown structures and branch patterns.

Old seedless cones remain on trees for years, often next to new cones.

Larix gmelinii var. *japonica*
GMELIN LARCH

This species is named after Johann Georg Gmelin, a famous German-Russian botanist and explorer of the Siberian forests, who lived from 1709 to 1755. It is also known as the Kurile (or Dahurian) Larch; but the Kurile Island Chain in eastern Russia is just a tiny part of the enormous natural area of this species.

Female cones become ripe in one growing season, and release seeds in late summer. Pale brown cones remain on the tree for a long time.

WINDSWEPT EFFECT

"A rather odd tree, but well suited to the small home garden because it doesn't grow too big," wrote A.R. Buckley, former Curator of the Arboretum, in 1965. "Like the symbolic Japanese tree its branches rise in a complete horizontal plane. The top looks as if it had been cut short so that the tree presents a kind of windswept effect. In fall the leaves of the tree turn to a luminous yellow, a brilliance that lasts for three or four weeks."

With its irregular branching patterns and bright yellow needles in the fall, the Gmelin Larch is a valued tree in landscape architecture in cold climates. One of these striking trees can be seen in the Circle area, close to the Arboretum entrance. Planted in 1887 and leaning a little, it is one of the original trees of the Arboretum.

Soft, light green needles turn yellow and fall off every autumn.

A VERY HARDY TREE FOR COLD CLIMATES

Gmelin Larch forests cover huge areas in north-eastern Russia. Together with the Siberian Larch, it forms the most extensive forest type on earth. The Gmelin Larch tree withstands extremely cold Arctic winters and successfully regenerates on permafrost soils during the few months of an Arctic summer.

The Gmelin Larch grows quickly and becomes a large tree under favourable conditions. On more harsh sites it is a short, knotty tree.

Bark is coarse with corky scales on old trees.

Needing full sun, shade from spruce or pines can suppress its growth in warmer areas.

Wood of the Gmelin Larch is very durable and heavy, so that it does not float. The Gmelin Larch does not face dangerous pests and diseases when cultivated. It is a very cold-hardy tree, but can be damaged by early spring frosts if new growth has started.

The crown is transparent, and conical or asymmetric with very long branches.

k. gier

Larix occidentalis

WESTERN LARCH

"The Western Larch" wrote A.R. Buckley, Curator of the Arboretum in 1965, "is most spectacular in the spring, when its long, soft, green leaves attain their full length and the exquisite, newly formed pink cones provide a pleasing contrast."

As with other larch trees, the Western Larch has two types of shoots: long and short. Both types of shoots lose their soft needles every fall.

THE TALLEST, MOST MAGNIFICENT LARCH

The Western Larch is the tallest and perhaps the most magnificent of all larch species, reaching a height of 30 to 60 metres. Growing in the interior mountains of western North America, it matches the size of its giant forest neighbours: the Douglas-fir, Ponderosa Pine, Western Hemlock, Grand Fir and Western Red Cedar.

A Western Larch planted in 1909 can be seen at the north end of the Circle area of the Arboretum. The beauty of this tree, high and narrow in the dawn sky (see photo), illustrates why it has been used as an ornamental tree outside its natural range. It is a healthy tree in park settings, but does not tolerate shade at any age. While the best Western Larch will grow on deep, moist soils, these trees tolerate both dry and wet sites.

Western Larch wood is strong, dense and durable. It is the most important native larch for pulpwood production and lumber. Western Larch seeds are eaten by birds and small animals. Other parts of the tree are rarely consumed by deer or rabbits.

Western Larch trees grow quickly for the first 100 years and then live a few centuries more, mainly increasing their trunk diameter.

Its bark is very thick. The outer corky layer can be up to one foot thick on large, old trees.

Female cones (left) grow in any direction: upward or downward. Seed bracts are longer than the wooded cone scales.

The lower photo shows both male (little yellow) and female cones.

The Western Larch crown is relatively tall and narrow.

kigier

Larix sibirica

SIBERIAN LARCH

Like other larch trees, there are two types of shoot, long and short, both of which lose their soft needles every fall. The long shoots are one year old; the short ones are older.

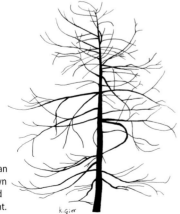

The Siberian Larch crown is light and transparent.

k.Gier

"In Siberian tradition, God made two trees at the creation: a female, the fir; and a male, the larch. The larch is one of the few trees that grows in the tundra, where a group of seven or more is considered to be a sacred grove." FRED HAGENEDER, 2005

First planted in the Arboretum in 1896, mature Siberian Larches can be found at the centre of the Circle area. While their needles and cones resemble those of the European Larch, the cones on the Siberian Larch tend to hang in long clusters. The crown is light and transparent, without the wide, horizontal branches of the European Larch, nor the tall, narrow appearance of the Western Larch.

FROM COLD FORESTS TO PARK SETTINGS

The Siberian Larch was introduced to North America from Russia where larch forests account for one of the highest portions of forested land. As well as growing on permafrost soils, Siberian Larch is the sole survivor on a variety of infertile sites in the mountains of western Siberia. In old, mixed forests occurring on more fertile soils, Siberian Larch does not survive in the shade of spruce, pine and fir. It is now a common ornamental specimen in European and North American parks, generally healthy, as long as it gets sunlight.

Wood of the Siberian Larch is strong and durable, but too heavy for many applications in the lumber and construction industries. Like other larch logs, it does not float. Every few years, Siberian Larch trees produce an abundant crop of seeds, edible for birds and small animals.

The Siberian Larch grows quickly when it is young and when planted on good soil. It never becomes a tall, massive tree. Needles change colour before falling from the tree.

Bark is thin and coarse on old trees.

Male and female cones grow on the same twigs (far left). Female cones are reddish when young, greenish when mature (above).

Syringa reticulata

JAPANESE TREE LILAC

The Japanese Tree Lilac is a gracefully shaped tree with creamy white flower trusses, deep green leaves, bright brown bark and bronzy seed pods which in early winter "gleam like golden candelabras in the sun." These decorative features appealed to A. R. Buckley, former Curator of the Arboretum, who called this species "…one of the best trees for growing in small gardens."

There are four Japanese Tree Lilacs in the Arboretum; one is in the maple area, the others are further south along the path. The oldest was planted in 1905. Another 56 Japanese Tree Lilacs can be seen around the Farm. Four were planted in 1921 alongside the gazebo in the Ornamental Gardens, and these tower above the other lilacs in that location.

Opposite, simple leaves show prominent veins on top and underneath.

GREAT ORNAMENTAL VALUE

Japanese Tree Lilacs originated in northern Japan. As do all lilacs, they need well-drained, fertile soil and full sun to become healthy, blooming trees. The small, relatively scarce trees have no commercial lumber value, but their ornamental value and cold-hardiness have made Japanese Tree Lilacs attractive to landscape designers around the world. The more upright selection, 'Ivory Silk', is very popular in Ottawa.

Bees and other nectar hunters are attracted to Japanese Tree Lilacs during the two to three weeks of blooming. Other parts of the tree have little value to wildlife, and no serious pests or diseases attack the tree in parks or on lawns. Some borers, powdery mildew, and blights damage Japanese Tree Lilacs when growing in the shade, or when stressed by pollution.

Twigs are thin, but on the ends bear big, upright clusters of perfect (bisexual), four-petalled flowers.

Bark is smooth, thin and glossy unless it is very old. Large, conspicuous lenticels (corky spots) are a feature.

After pollination, flowers become capsules with small seeds in late summer. Open, empty capsules remain on trees over the winter.

fyi *A Japanese Tree Lilac grows slowly, even on good sites. It takes a few decades to grow 10 m high.*

The tree is single- or multi-stemmed. Both forms have stiff, upright branches forming a dense, rounded crown.

Tilia platyphyllos
BIGLEAF LINDEN

Alternate, simple leaves are heart-shaped with dense, short hairs underneath.

The Bigleaf Linden, a native of Europe, is known as Large-leaved Lime in Britain. The North American native linden (*Tilia americana*) is called Basswood. The wide-spreading tree in the photo and drawing can be found just north of the old Botany Building (#74) at the entrance to the Arboretum. A collection of magnificent, large linden trees is across the path from the old Windbreak at the northeastern end of the Arboretum next to the railway tracks.

A FAMILIAR SIGHT ON CITY STREETS

The Bigleaf Linden is rarely found in the wild in North America but is a valued tree in parks, gardens and on streets for its shade and attractive shape. The tree tolerates urban pollution and soil compaction. Many ornamental cultivars have been developed, some of which may be subject to disease or pests.

Young trees survive growing in shade and mature trees live a long time if they get the full sun they need. Bigleaf Linden wood is scarce and used mostly for wood carving and decorating.

A HAVEN FOR BIRDS AND SMALL ANIMALS

Much loved by birds and small animals, the Bigleaf Linden provides nutritious leaves, sweet flowers, edible fruits and choice nesting sites.

Yellowish flowers grow in small clusters on a long stalk attached to a long, narrow leaflet (or bract).

Seeds, enclosed by woody shells, become mature in one season but, buried in topsoil, they stay dormant for many years.

Rough, flat-ridged bark covers the trunk and low branches of mature trees. The bark is smooth on younger trees.

k.gier

The Bigleaf Linden has a wide crown of many arching branches.

Ginkgo biloba
GINKGO *or* MAIDENHAIR TREE

"This strange tree, a link with prehistoric times, is so vastly different from other plants that it rates a story of its own."
A.R. BUCKLEY, FORMER CURATOR OF THE ARBORETUM

fyi *The Ginkgo has been on this earth since the time of the dinosaurs.*

The Ginkgo or Maidenhair tree first came to the attention of European botanists as a fossil plant that was a contemporary of dinosaurs in North America, Europe, and Asia. The first live Ginkgo was brought from Japan to Europe in the early 18th century by Engelbert Kaempfer, a German physician and botanist.

Natural habitats of the Ginkgo are unknown. The trees have been cultivated on monastery and temple grounds for at least a millennium. It is a very adaptable tree, surviving huge environmental changes and evolution of ecosystems over millions of years.

The Ginkgo is now a popular ornamental tree, and many cultivars have recently been developed for use in modern, environment-friendly architectural designs. It requires little care except for cleaning up after an abundant seed crop. It is cold-hardy, pest-free and resistant to city pollutants.

AN EARLY ATTRACTION AT THE ARBORETUM
Among the first trees planted at the Farm, the Ginkgo had proved hardy in Ottawa by 1896. In 1924, Mr. W.T. Macoun, former Dominion Horticulturist, suggested that "it is such a striking and attractive tree that it should be much more generally planted than it is." This advice appears to have been heeded as many young and mature Ginkgos now grow in Ottawa.

The Ginkgo in the photo and drawing is on the Campus lawn across from the Macoun Memorial Garden. Other mature trees grow in the Circle area.

Fan-shaped leaves, resembling the leaflets on maidenhair ferns, turn yellow in autumn and fall from the tree shortly thereafter. In the fall, the tree "glows with a soft, luminous yellow tone, " as A.R. Buckley observed.

Bark of old trees is coarse and flat ridged.

First green, then bright yellow, the cherry-like "fruit" can be abundant in early fall. Female trees produce viable seeds if male trees grow nearby.

Ginkgos are large trees in terms of the diameter of their trunk or multiple trunks, but rarely grow tall.

Bunches of leaves grow on short shoots (as in the photo), while alternate, single leaves grow on long, one-year-old shoots.

The crown of the Ginkgo is long, narrow and transparent, consisting mainly of straight, thin branches.

k.gier

Magnolia acuminata
CUCUMBER TREE

Cucumber Tree flowers are big with many pistils and stamens, a characteristic of the oldest flowering plants in history.

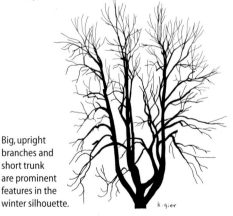

Big, upright branches and short trunk are prominent features in the winter silhouette.

k.gier

Attractive foliage and a handsome winter silhouette are key features of the Cucumber Tree, rather than its large flowers, which are not as showy as those of other magnolia species. Its common name comes from the cylindrical fruit pod which, when green, resembles a cucumber. The large old Cucumber Tree in the photo and drawing can be seen near the William Saunders Building in the Campus area of the Farm. A young specimen, planted in 1997, is coming along nicely in the magnolia area of the Arboretum.

ENDANGERED IN CANADA

Cucumber Trees grow naturally in the moist deciduous forests of North America west of the Appalachian Mountains. They are the only magnolias native to Canada, where they are an endangered species. They occur in southern Ontario as minor trees in oak and Sugar Maple stands. In the southern U.S., they appear with oaks, hickories, and other magnolia trees. Cucumber Trees need moist, fertile soils and are prone to frost damage.

AN EXCELLENT SHADE TREE

The very ornamental Cucumber Tree is an excellent shade tree and decorates parks and residential properties well north of its natural range in North America. It rarely suffers from pests and diseases, but can be damaged by spring frosts, summer droughts and urban pollution.

A drug used in heart surgery was first isolated from the bark of this tree. The wood is soft and durable, with many uses in the lumber and furniture industries. The seeds of the Cucumber Tree are eaten by birds and small animals.

Bark is thin and furrowed on old trees. Corky outer flakes are very soft.

The crown of the Cucumber Tree is wide and dense when it is exposed to full sun. In the forest, it is a tall tree with a narrow crown. Large, silky buds (left) are noticeable on twig ends.

Fruits consist of many red seeds individually encased in a thin capsule. When green, they resemble cucumbers. This photo was taken elsewhere in Ottawa, where the climate is far from optimum for magnolia trees to produce seeds and propagate themselves.

Alternate, simple leaves turn yellow-bronze in fall.

Magnolia salicifolia

ANISE MAGNOLIA

"When I mention magnolias for eastern Canada to non-gardening acquaintances they look at me and smile. They just will not believe that this kind of plant could possibly leave its Southern Georgia mansions and survive in our frigid climate." A.R. BUCKLEY, FORMER CURATOR OF THE ARBORETUM, 1966

Mr. Buckley was not referring to the great Southern Magnolia (*M. grandiflora*) but "several equally beautiful magnolias, which, although deciduous, will grow in the milder parts of eastern Canada and produce the magnificent blooms for which the plants are so well noted."

One outstanding specimen in the Arboretum's magnolia collection is the early blooming Anise Magnolia, named for the scent of its crushed leaves and stems. It is also known as Willow-leafed Magnolia because of its relatively narrow leaves, which give the tree a finer texture than its neighbours.

At the ends of stiff, vigorously growing twigs are silky flower buds. (right) Perfect flowers (above) with six long, white petals appear in spring, before the leaves.

GROWING NATURALLY ONLY IN JAPAN

The natural range of the Anise Magnolia is limited to remnants of virgin beech forests on foggy mountain slopes of the northern islands of Japan. It does not compete with the tallest trees there, but is abundant in forest glades. Anise Magnolia trees prefer rich, moist soil and high air humidity.

This spectacular tree is widely grown in arboreta, parks and on European and North American city streets. Specimens and cultivars are also popular as focal points on private lawns or front yards.

Seeds of the Anise Magnolia are consumed by birds in the fall. As with other magnolia, it suffers from many pests and diseases. Rotten stems are common problems and it also suffers from dieback after very cold winters. Flowers can be affected by spring frosts.

Anise Magnolia trees grow slowly and retain their compact, dense crowns for most of their life span.

kqier

In early spring, the whole Anise Magnolia tree is covered by flowers, replaced later by leaves.

The elongated fruit is composed of many individually encased seeds. Both fruit and seeds are reddish when ripe.

Bark remains thin and smooth for many years. It becomes coarse on old trees, but is still thin.

Alternate leaves with tapered bases and tips emerge from numerous hairless buds. The hairless buds distinguish this magnolia from the similar Kobus Magnolia.

Magnolia fraseri
FRASER MAGNOLIA

The three Fraser Magnolias are the tallest of the magnolias in the collection at the Arboretum, with the exception of the Cucumber Tree. Their elegant and beautiful, creamy white flowers should not be missed. These flowers appear later than the white ones of the neighbouring Kobus and Anise Magnolias and are often high up on the trees, hidden by the huge Fraser Magnolia leaves.

Adjacent to the Fraser Magnolias are examples of another fabulous magnolia species, the Umbrella Magnolia (*Magnolia tripetala*). If the Fraser Magnolia leaves are huge, those of the Umbrella Magnolia are giants, up to 90 cm long. Because of the size of the leaves, you have to be some distance away to see the magnificent white flowers.

NAMED AFTER JOHN FRASER, A SCOTTISH BOTANIST

Fraser Magnolia is a North American tree with a very small range in the mid-south Appalachian Mountains; hence, another name for it is Mountain Magnolia. Quaker botanists William Bartram and his son John discovered the tree growing in Georgia in 1775, and named it for a Scottish botanist John Fraser. It is a minor component in hardwood forests of Sugar Maple, beech, and Yellow Buckeye. Fraser Magnolia trees need well-drained, fertile soils. Excess moisture can limit their growth.

Flowers are perfect with several long, creamy white petals, and hundreds of stamens and pistils in the middle. Alternately arranged leaves grow mostly on the ends of peripheral twigs and branches. Leaves are simple and large, with ears at the base.

Its wood, of relatively poor quality, has only minor value as lumber and pulpwood. Much greater demand for Fraser Magnolia trees arises from the needs of green architecture and ornamental landscaping. With its showy flowers and leaves, the tree is well known far from its natural range. Growing in parks and on small lawns, it produces abundant flowers when exposed to full sun.

The Fraser Magnolia tree grows fast, especially from stump sprouts, and has a short life. The crown is oval with several wide-spreading limbs. Twigs are stout.

Bark is thin and smooth on trees of all sizes.

Cucumber-like fruit contains many individually-wrapped seeds. Both fruit and seeds are red when ripe.

Forest animals munch on small Fraser Magnolia trees. Old trees are used for nests and dens, and the fruit is eaten by wildlife. Fraser Magnolia has many pests and diseases, the most dangerous of which are fungi causing rot on stems and trunks. It is prone to damage from winter and urban pollution.

Magnolia kobus

KOBUS MAGNOLIA

In spring before any leaves appear, perfect flowers with several long, white petals emerge from the buds.

Alternate leaves have a narrow base and short stalk.

Magnolias are among the most beautiful landscape plants. Increasingly popular in Ottawa, their principal attraction is spectacular, large flowers. Magnolias come in a variety of sizes, forms and textures, evident in the collection at the Arboretum, particularly Kobus Magnolia. *The Living Collection of the Dominion Arboretum* (Douglas, 2005) includes Kobus Magnolia and six varieties including *borealis* and *stellata*.

The Arboretum collection is not new. Experimentation began with six species of magnolia, including *Magnolia kobus*, planted in the Arboretum in the years 1896-97. Winter kill caused some species to be rated as "tender" at Ottawa, but the collection has survived with the oldest tree, an Umbrella Magnolia (*M. tripetala*), planted in 1907. Most are about 40 years old. The oldest Kobus Magnolia dates from 1952.

PURE WHITE FLOWERS AND CLEAN, SPARKLING LEAVES

The Kobus Magnolia, also known as Northern Japanese Magnolia, grows in the riparian forests of Japan and southern Korea. The Katsura Tree is the prime species in those habitats; magnolia is only a minor component. Rich, moist soils and no dry seasons are needed for the Kobus Magnolia to grow large.

With its pure white flowers and clean, sparkling leaves, it has had a long history of use for ornamental purposes in Japan. Wood of the Kobus Magnolia has also been used there for making utensils and for firewood. Seeds were first brought to England in 1879 but did not flower for about 30 years. Regular specimens and cultivars were introduced to parks and cities all around the world during the 20th century.

The Kobus Magnolia can also be seen on private front lawns or yards. Grafted trees

The Kobus Magnolia grows slowly, taking a few decades to mature. Multiple stems and wide-spreading branches are common features of this tree. The winter silhouette is similar to that of Anise Magnolia. Twigs are stout with large hairy buds on their ends (right).

produce flowers at a much younger age than trees grown from seeds, but both need full sun to bloom. Birds consume the seeds of the Kobus Magnolia in fall. As with other magnolias, pests and diseases pose many threats. Rotten stems and winter dieback are common problems.

Elongated fruit contain many individually enveloped seeds. Both fruit and seeds are reddish when ripe.

Bark is thin and smooth for many years. On old trees it becomes coarse and furrowed, but remains thin.

"The familiar leaves have become the symbol of the Canadian nation; the running of the sap is a sign of spring and of youth, and the flaming colours of its autumn foliage mark the passage of time." (Harris, 2003)

From the very beginning of the Arboretum, there has been a large collection of maples, both native and exotic, from the bushy and scrubby types to the tall and perfectly proportioned. In 1904, there were 122 species and varieties, many of which were in the maple area south of the main entrance. The collection remains large, with 96 species and varieties in 2005 (Douglas, 2005), still mostly in the maple area.

Nine maple species are included in this book. Five Ornamental maples from abroad follow this introduction: the Miyabe Maple (*Acer miyabei*), Norway Maple (*A. platanoides*), Sycamore Maple (*A. pseudoplatanus*), Tatarian Maple (*A. tataricum*) and Purpleblow Maple (*A. truncatum*).

Our beautiful native Red Maple (*A. rubrum*), Silver Maple (*A. saccharinum*) and Sugar Maple (*A. saccharum*) are all highly valued as Resource trees, and are found on pages 146, 148 and 150, respectively. One native maple, the Manitoba Maple (*A. negundo*), is included with the Environmental group, on page 226.

Top: Norway Maple 'Goldsworth Purple'
Above: Silver Maple 'Wieri Laciniatum' (in Ornamental Gardens)
Right: Manitoba Maple flowers, Norway Maple seeds
Opposite: Red and Sugar Maples

Acer miyabei
MIYABE MAPLE

fyi Leaves turn bright yellow in fall, unlike most North American maples.

Opposite leaves are deeply cut into three to five lobes. The tree's samaras or keys are always in pairs with wings which form an almost straight line.

Limited to isolated islands or valleys in northern Japan, the Miyabe Maple is rarely seen in North America, either in arboreta or parks. It is named after Kingo Miyabe, a Japanese botanist and explorer of forests in Japan, China and far eastern regions of Russia in the late 19th and early 20th centuries.

A RARE SPECIES

The only specimen in the Arboretum of this little-known species is an old tree in the maple section, planted in the mid 1890s. In 1895, Mr. W.T. Macoun, Foreman of Forestry at the time, recorded that 179 species and varieties of trees and shrubs that were new to the collection at Ottawa had been donated by the Arnold Arboretum at Boston, Massachusetts. Perhaps a more likely origin of the Miyabe Maple was a donation of seeds of Japanese trees and shrubs in 1896 by the Royal Botanic Gardens of Sapporo, Japan. Other notable donors in that year were the Royal Gardens at Kew, England, and the Botanic Gardens at Ventimiglia, Italy.

LATER TO LEAF THAN OTHER MAPLES IN THE ARBORETUM

The Miyabe Maple grows naturally along river banks. In cultivation, however, the Miyabe Maple can tolerate drought better than the Norway Maple (*Acer platanoides*) and is also considered hardier than the Field Maple (*Acer campestre*). It resists pollution and other city stresses. It is a slow growing tree and, in the Arboretum, comes into leaf later in the spring than the other maple species around it.

Miyabe Maple wood is unavailable on the market. This tree is not threatened by dangerous diseases or pests, and winter damage is insignificant. Small rodents forage on its flowers and fruits as they do on other maples.

The Miyabe Maple's bark is brown-grey and scaly, and relatively thin, even on big trees.

When in a sunny location, the Miyabe Maple forms a wide crown with big lower branches.

Clusters of small flowers appear on outer parts of the crown at the same time as the leaves.

Most twigs grow upright and many of them remain alive on inner parts of the crown for years.

k.gier

Acer platanoides
NORWAY MAPLE

Opposite, simple, lobed leaves grow on long stalks and release a milky sap if broken. In fall, the bright green leaves will turn to bright yellow. Pairs of widely spread, winged seeds fly from the trees in late summer.

The crown is very dense and low if the tree occupies a sunny position.

k.gier

The Norway Maple grows quickly into a large ornamental tree. It comes in many varieties, 22 of which were in the Arboretum in 2005, according to *The Living Collection of the Dominion Arboretum* (Douglas, 2005). W.T. Macoun, former Dominion Horticulturist, referred in 1897 to the very striking 'Schwedleri' variety with its attractive shade of purple, a fine example of which can be seen near Birch Drive. The purple-leafed cultivar in the photo is similar in appearance to the 'Schwedleri' and, along with other mature Norway Maples, is found in the maple area.

MATURE NORWAY MAPLES
CAST A HEAVY SHADOW

Norway Maples are common in European temperate forests beneath oak, beech, or ash trees. Young Norway Maples grow well in the shade of mature oaks, but mature Norway Maples cast a heavy shade in which other trees find it difficult to flourish. They avoid extremes related to either dry, sandy or wet, clayish sites and grow best on fertile, moist uplands.

A very popular ornamental tree, the Norway Maple and its cultivars grow in parks, on streets and private properties throughout Europe and eastern North America. The cultivar named 'Globosum' does not have the massive crown and extensive root system of the species, so it can be used where damage to buildings and utility lines is an issue.

PROVIDES DURABLE FLOOR WOOD

The hard, fine-grained wood of the Norway Maple is used for floors and furniture. Flowers and seeds provide food for wildlife. Dangerous diseases and pests are not a threat, but the tree is susceptible to winter frost.

Flowers are upright and appear in clusters before the leaves. Each flower has five small petals and five sepals.

Dark grey bark gives an impression of smoothness, even on old trees which have narrow, low furrows.

Norway Maples grow quickly and in 30 to 40 years produce a large, rounded crown consisting of many big limbs. In the photo is 'Goldsworth Purple'.

Acer pseudoplatanus
SYCAMORE MAPLE

As with many maples, five-lobed leaves have distinctive, deeply engraved veins and a heart shaped base.

In parks they are smaller but are still large trees with dense wide crowns.

k. gier

A handsome old Sycamore Maple in the maple area beside the Circle road, is the only mature tree of the species in the Arboretum. It has weathered a lot of winters that are colder than it prefers. First planted in the Arboretum in 1890, the Sycamore Maple species was rated as "half hardy" in 1899. Some varieties were killed back to ground level during severe winters.

Hot weather and dry soils are less of a problem for the Sycamore Maple than cold climates and poor soil. It grows naturally in temperate mixed forests in Europe and western Asia, alongside oak, beech, spruce, linden and other forest giants.

MANY USES FOR LANDSCAPING

Similar in size and habit to the Norway Maple, it has a broad, arching, attractive shape and has many uses for landscaping, from borders on busy city streets to adding shape and beauty to spacious park settings. Leaves of the Sycamore Maple resemble those of the Sycamore or Plane tree; hence its Latin name, which means "false Plane".

Strong and hard Sycamore Maple wood is prized by veneer and furniture makers. The tree's flowers and seeds feed squirrels, chipmunks, and birds. Dense crowns on the trees supply good nesting places. The species does not suffer from dangerous diseases in parks, but in other locations may suffer from a canker that girdles and kills the stems or branches.

Sycamore Maples can reach over 30 m high and can live a few hundred years in their native habitats.

Loose, corky scales and smooth inner bark create an irregular mosaic on the trunks and limbs of mature trees.

Big greenish buds are noticeable in winter on vigorous twigs. Small green-yellow flowers appear in big hanging clusters when leaves are well developed.

Many pairs of winged seeds remain in clusters on trees until late summer or fall.

Acer tataricum

TATARIAN MAPLE

Leaves have three shallow lobes and an elongated shape, which is uncommon among maples.

Because of its hardiness and colourful fall leaves, the Tatarian Maple was considered by W.T. Macoun, former Dominion Horticulturist, to be a very valuable small ornamental tree, especially for locations where there are few hardy species available. An old Tatarian Maple can be seen in the Arboretum's maple area, near where the southern path meets the Circle road. It has colour and ornamental value, not only in the fall, but also in summer, with its red-green seeds and compact crown.

In Europe and North America, Tatarian Maple specimens and cultivars are commonly seen on streets, in parks and as hedges.

A SMALL, ORNAMENTAL TREE, EASY TO GROW

The Tatarian Maple is native to Europe and Asia where it grows in dry, deciduous forests. It is a small tree, often multi-stemmed, and forms a dense layer under oaks. This species tolerates a variety of soils and survives in very cold climates. Its wood is strong, but the small stems are usually only used locally for firewood.

Flowers and seeds of the Tatarian Maple feed small rodents and birds. The species does not experience dangerous pests and diseases and is easy to grow in small yards, under utility lines, and near houses. Pruning of old stems is needed to rejuvenate aging trees and, on fertile sites, it may be necessary to control the many seedlings, which emerge from countless viable seeds.

When leaves are well developed, small green-yellow flowers appear in rounded upright clusters.

k.gier

The crown is compact and dense because of many small branches and twigs.

ORNAMENTAL

Many pairs of winged seeds (samaras) are red-green most of the summer, becoming brown in fall when fully mature.

Stems (or trunks) of all ages have thin grey bark which becomes corkier with age. Trees may be re-born from sprouts on stumps.

Tatarian Maple is a fast growing, short living tree.

Acer truncatum

PURPLEBLOW MAPLE

Simple palmate leaves have five sharp pointed lobes. Twigs are thin and rigid.

New growth on the Purpleblow Maple has a purplish colour; hence its common name. Another name for the tree is Shantung Maple, reflecting its origins in the forests of Manchuria and Korea, where it fills gaps among the taller oak, pine and fir trees.

The species was first planted in the Arboretum in 1897. A mature Purpleblow Maple, planted in 1934, can be seen in the maple section of the Arboretum by the Circle road, alongside old Sycamore and Tatarian Maple trees. It is a beautiful tree with a full rounded crown, tinged with purple in spring, and colourful orange leaves in the fall.

AN ORNAMENTAL TREE THAT IS RARELY USED

The Purpleblow Maple tree does best on moist slopes with deep, well-drained soil, but tolerates cold winters, heat, drought and a variety of soils. With these qualities and its ornamental value, extensive use in landscaping might be expected. Perhaps it is less readily available than the Norway Maple, which is similar in habit and frequently planted, but the Purpleblow Maple is rarely used by landscapers.

Wood of the Purpleblow Maple is hard and strong, but logs are small. The tree does not suffer from pests and diseases and is easy to maintain on small lawns and yards. Seeds, like those of other maples, are nutritious for birds and small animals.

Pairs of winged seeds remain on trees through summer into fall.

The Purpleblow Maple grows slowly throughout its life. The tree is small, even when mature, and has a wide, short trunk.

Bark is thin and smooth. Mature trees have a coarse, corky outer layer.

Clusters of small, perfect flowers appear on ends of twigs when leaves emerge.

Several big limbs form a rounded crown which casts heavy shade.

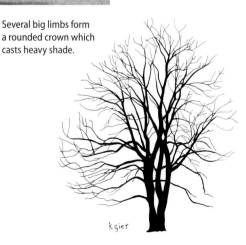

k.gier

Pinus peuce
BALKAN PINE

Needles are thin and soft, in bundles of five.

Seeds become mature at the end of the second growing season, large open cones remaining on the tree for a few years.

Also known as Macedonian Pine, this species was introduced to North America from its natural habitat in the Balkan Mountains. It is a very decorative pine with soft needles in bundles of five, a pyramidal form and large cones. When exposed to full sun, it develops a symmetrical, compact crown.

ONE OF THE BEST ORNAMENTAL EVERGREENS

The Balkan Pine makes an excellent ornamental tree on both small and large properties. It is very popular in Scandinavian parks and gardens, where it is known as Silk Pine, because of its silky foliage. There is one old specimen of Balkan Pine, planted in 1895, in the Circle area of the Arboretum.

Balkan Pine trees produce a lot of pollen each year. This caused a problem in the past at the Farm. A.R. Buckley in 1980 noted that most seeds sent out from the seed exchange labelled as Eastern White Pine seeds may have been hybrids from Balkan and Eastern White Pines.

TOLERATES A VARIETY OF GROWING CONDITIONS

Balkan Pines form pure stands of small trees at high elevations in the Balkan Mountains. On lower slopes and ridges, they are a component of spruce-fir forests. The Balkan Pine tolerates a variety of soils and growing conditions, including severe cold and wind, but does not accept clay or poor drainage. Its wood is strong and durable, but is rarely available.

Birds and small animals eat the seeds of this tree, the dense crown of which provides good nesting sites. It is resistant to White Pine Blister Rust but prone to damage from air pollution, and may be affected by other diseases and pests that attack the Eastern White Pine.

Balkan Pine trees grow slowly and steadily over decades.

Smooth resinous bark of a young tree becomes thick, consisting of flat plates.

After pollination, the cones turn green and release a whitish resin.

Those grown in the open have dense crowns and the ends of their branches tend to turn upward.

k.gier

Pinus ponderosa
PONDEROSA PINE

Before pollination, male and female cones are like those of other pines. At the end of the second growing season female cones release ripe seeds that are about 6 mm long; the seed wing being three times longer.

Long flexible needles grow in bunches of three at the top of thick twigs.

A long with other pines and spruce, Ponderosa Pines were planted at the end of the 19th century in the Windbreak at the eastern edge of the Arboretum, next to the railway track and tunnel. There is one old specimen in the Circle, which dates to 1887. No cultivars, varieties or subspecies grow in the Arboretum.

A "WEIGHTY" TREE
Ponderosa Pines are massive trees in their natural habitat. The name *ponderosa* means "weighty" and, because of their size, they are also known as Bull Pines. They are long-lived trees. Those growing in the western mountains live a few hundred years.

BEST IN COARSE, SANDY SOIL
The natural range of the Ponderosa Pine is western North America from southern British Columbia to northern Mexico. It will grow in different types of soil but grows best in coarse, sandy soil. The species has adapted to wildfire, the low-intensity forest fires which can occur every five years or so. A vigorous taproot allows the tree to tolerate strong winds and moisture deficiency.

On a hot day, it is said that the bark of the Ponderosa Pine smells like vanilla. Many birds and small mammals such as mice, chipmunks and squirrels eat the seeds of this pine. Squirrels also clip the cone-bearing twigs, destroying flowers and immature cones. Many insects and fungi attack the needles, cones, branches, bark and roots. However, no serious pest problems have been recorded in the Arboretum.

Ponderosa Pines, like this one in the old Windbreak, are tall with broad, conical crowns starting well above the ground. Trunks are often free of branches for most of their length.

Yellowish-brown rectangular scales form a very thick bark. It is because of this thick bark and clear (branchless) trunk that trees are able to survive ground fires.

Pinus rigida
PITCH PINE

The Pitch Pine in the photograph is in the Circle area of the Arboretum beside a clump of Smoketrees and two Korean Pines. Almost a hundred years old, it is an imposing specimen with its broad, pyramidal outline. Another Pitch Pine, also planted in 1908, is more crowded towards the centre of the Circle.

RARE IN OTHER PARTS OF CANADA

The only natural habitat in Canada for the Pitch Pine is near Ottawa, on the northeast shore of Lake Ontario and in the Thousand Islands area along the St. Lawrence River. The species also grows in the Appalachian Mountains and on the eastern plains of U.S.A. The size and growth of Pitch Pines varies according to location and soil quality. In the north, trees can be misshapen and gnarled, compared with a straighter form further south. They become large trees on good soils; small and slow-growing on cliffs or sandy outwashes and dunes.

Needles, in bundles of three, are long like those of white pines but twisted like those of the Jack Pine.

GOOD FOR REFORESTATION AND FOR LANDSCAPING ON BARE, SANDY SITES

The Pitch Pine is one of the first tree colonizers after large forest fires. Unlike other pines, the tree produces sprouts from dormant, fire-resistant buds on its trunk and branches. Pitch Pines produce seed cones at an early age and will re-establish the forest environment, after which white pines, hemlocks or oaks become dominant.

Pitch Pine wood is good for structural timbers and for pulp, but uses are limited as the wood is often of low quality due to knots and crooks. Pitch Pines need little soil moisture and

Seeds become mature in two years, but cones remain on the tree for many years.

The crown of the Pitch Pine is oval-shaped, often irregular with many short branches.

Scaly bark of young trees becomes thick and flat-plated with narrow deep furrows as the tree matures.

fertility and, thus, are very good for landscaping projects where there are poor soils and moisture extremes. The trees do not, however, tolerate shade.

Pitch Pine seeds support birds and rodent populations in parks and forests. There are no major disease and pest problems, but salt spray damages the needles.

Populus alba

WHITE POPLAR

Simple leaves are triangular with lobes. The top is dark green; the bottom white and woolly.

The crown is pyramidal on young trees. On trees that are 50 years of age or more, such as this one in the Arboretum, the crown becomes rounded or irregular.

k. giey

A handsome White Poplar has been growing beside the road in the Circle area for over a hundred years. A.R. Buckley, former Curator of the Arboretum, wrote in 1980 that this species is "a distinctive poplar because of the white woolly undersurfaces of its leaves, which the slightest breeze reveals as shining silver. When the tree is mature, the main trunk is dark grey and beautifully fissured, but the extending large branches are almost as white as those of the canoe birch (*Betula papyrifera*)."

Close to the old White Poplar on the Circle road is a young Silver Poplar (*Populus alba* 'Nivea'). This is "a beautiful form of the White Poplar, the leaves having more intense silvery undersides" (Buckley, 1980).

ORNAMENTAL AND USEFUL FOR REFORESTATION

White Poplar is native to most of Europe and western Asia and was among the first tree species to be introduced to North America from Europe. It grows in deciduous forests at the early stages of reforestation, predominantly on bottomlands in river valleys. Willows and other poplars grow on the same sites, but White Poplar trees tolerate drier soils.

The decorative appearance of its leaves and its ability to grow quickly on various soils make this tree very attractive both for green architecture and for site reclamation in areas often completely devoid of forested lands. Wood of the White Poplar is soft and brittle, and of value only where other woods are scarce.

White Poplar has some food value for wildlife. Because of their brittle wood, these trees may suffer damage from wind and ice storms, and broken branches are then prone to rot. Cottony seeds may be messy on streets or in parks: the simple solution — plant more male trees.

Like all poplar species, White Poplar trees grow quickly. Both big and small branches grow upright, creating a somewhat dense crown.

Male and female flowers grow on separate trees and are gathered in similar-looking catkins. Flowering and pollination occur before leaves come out. Like those on other poplars, female catkins produce millions of cottony seeds, which fly off the trees in early summer.

Bark is thin, smooth, and light grey-green. Some dark spots and cracks appear on old, thick trunks.

Picea pungens
COLORADO SPRUCE

Pale brown, mature seed-bearing cones are noticeable on upper branches in late summer and fall. Seeds have been released from these cones (on *Picea pungens* 'Hoopsii').

The beauty of the Colorado Spruce makes it a very popular ornamental tree in North America and Europe. First planted in the Arboretum in 1889, this tree from the Rocky Mountains proved to be perfectly hardy in Ottawa.

A VARIETY OF COLOURS

Mature Colorado Spruce trees are found in the spruce grove of the Circle directly across from the Hosta Garden. Attractive specimens of the species and its varieties can be seen elsewhere in the Arboretum. *The Living Collection of the Dominion Arboretum* (Douglas, 2005) lists 8 varieties, including Koster Blue Spruce, a very popular ornamental. The first Koster Blue Spruce in the Arboretum was obtained from Spaeth's nursery in Germany and planted in 1898. Another variety, Silver Colorado Spruce, is captured in the drawing.

Colorado Spruce originates on cool, moist slopes and valley bottoms in the central and southern Rocky Mountains. It can be a dominant tree or may be scattered throughout mixed forests of Douglas-fir, White Fir, and Engelmann Spruce. Colorado Spruce often grows on fresh sand and gravel deposits. Because of its shallow roots, it needs sites which preserve moisture close to the surface throughout the growing season. Colorado Spruce wood is brittle, knotty and resinous. Commercial supplies are not plentiful anywhere within its natural range.

Colorado Spruce trees provide excellent nesting and den sites for birds and small animals. Seeds are edible, but needles are unpalatable for wildlife. Spruce Spider Mites or canker (caused by a fungus) may damage or even kill trees, although these problems have not affected those in the Arboretum.

fyi *Colorado Spruce trees steadily increase the height of their dense conical crown while keeping lower branches close to the ground.*

Needles have four distinctive ridges. They are sharply pointed and remain on twigs for up to 5 years.

Bark is scaly, but it is often hidden from view by many horizontal twigs.

The tree flattens at the top at maturity and appears as a tall column for decades. The specimen captured below is a Silver Colorado Spruce (*Picea pungens* f. *argentea*).

Female cones are reddish before pollination, and then turn green. Male cones are inconspicuous, scattered on peripheral twigs between needles.

Platanus occidentalis
SYCAMORE

The shape of the leaf resembles those of the maple, but the Sycamore leaf arrangement is alternate.

fyi *Wood of the Sycamore is heavy and hard, used for making furniture, veneer, and for interior finishing.*

k.gier

Trees develop massive trunks, such as on this landmark Sycamore in the Ornamental Gardens, which has a wide spreading crown.

The Sycamore fits a variety of landscaping projects where a large and handsome focal tree is required. It has the largest girth of any North American deciduous tree and can reach five or six hundred years of age. Many urban plantings are of the London Plane Tree, *Platanus ×acerifolia*, a hybrid of *P. occidentalis* and *P. orientalis*. The London Plane Tree is chosen because of its greater resistance to disease.

A LANDMARK IN THE ORNAMENTAL GARDENS

The Sycamore species, also known as American Plane and Buttonwood, was first planted in the Arboretum in 1893. A giant specimen, planted in 1897, stands near the Macoun Memorial Garden in the Ornamental Gardens. Younger ones can be seen at the northern and southern ends near Prince of Wales Drive, as well as in the Campus area.

The Sycamore has large leaves which are late appearing in the spring and which are similar in shape to the leaves of the Sycamore Maple. Another striking feature is the natural peeling of its bark, which makes the tree look as though it "had withstood the onslaught of a thousand cannon." (Buckley, 1980)

The Sycamore is native to eastern North America, occurring in valleys on rich, moist sites created by the flooding and sedimentary deposits of rivers.

The Sycamore feeds and hosts many insects and fungi, which makes it prone to disease and pest problems. The most dangerous threat is Anthracnose, a disease which damages the leaves in early summer. This loss of leaves saps the strength of the tree and aggravates other problems. On healthy trees, intense root growth close to the surface may damage driveways or walkways.

The Sycamore grows quickly, reaching a height of over 30 m.

The bark on old trees is coarse and grey. On young trees it has whitish and greenish patches.

Male and female flowers grow separately on the same tree. Small ball-like heads of flowers appear the same time as leaves.

Dense, dry fruit consist of many small seeds. Fruit remain on a Sycamore tree well after the leaves have fallen.

RESOURCE TREES

Many of the 22 Resource trees in this book have proven to have valuable Ornamental, Fruit, or Environmental uses, but are included in the category of Resource trees because of their importance to industry. About 120 years ago, when the Dominion Arboretum was established, Ottawa was a busy lumber market with millions of board-feet of white pine going to Europe. Like the white pine in the 1880s in Ottawa, some of the Resource trees here are vital for lumber markets today. Others have become important in other forest product industries, such as the manufacture of pulp and paper, and fine furniture.

The Ottawa Valley region is forest land, by climate and structure. Following the age of the glaciers, the Ottawa Valley region was covered by mixed forests where both conifer and deciduous trees flourished. Old growth stands consisted of giant Eastern White Pine, American Beech, White Spruce, Eastern

Left: American Beech
Top, left: Silver Maple leaves
Top, right: White Ash seeds
Above: American Beech nuts

Hemlock, and White and Red Ash trees. Shorter trees, such as Red and Sugar Maples, Balsam Fir, Yellow Birch, Basswood and Ironwood, made a dense shade that allowed only a few species of shrubs and other plants to survive.

Shady woods can remain unchanged for hundreds of years unless ravaged by fire. Jack and Red Pines, Paper Birch and poplars take advantage of such fires. They colonize burnt areas and rapidly build a light canopy to shelter new generations of shade tolerant forest giants.

Other Resource trees originate in rolling hills, bogs, lakeshores and ravines. Eastern White Cedar, Tamarack, Hackberry and Silver Maple dominate in such areas and add their distinctive colours and textures to the Arboretum.

INSIGHT INTO THE FUTURE

In the forest belts at the Farm, experiments began in 1888 to test the resource potential of a variety of tree species. By 1901, a total of 23,300 trees were growing in belts of 2.8 kilometres along the northern and western perimeters. A small section of forest belt remains today, at the northern end of Fisher Avenue. Individual tree specimens of the species tested can also be seen in the Arboretum.

Who knows which tree will have the highest resource value in the Ottawa region in the 2080s? Perhaps it will be the Black Cherry, so rarely seen in Ottawa, or another of the hundreds of tree species recently seen growing at the Farm. The Arboretum's living collection shows us the past and gives us the future.

RESOURCE

Fraxinus americana

WHITE ASH

Leaves are compound, growing opposite in pairs. Male and female flowers grow on separate trees (see the European Ash for similar flowers).

Ash trees were among the first to be planted in the Arboretum. Huge old White and Red Ash trees can be seen in the open area of the Circle. The White Ash in the photo was planted in 1889. By 1904, there were 86 species and varieties of ash being tested in the Arboretum. In 2005, there were 35 species and varieties listed in *The Living Collection of the Dominion Arboretum* (Douglas, 2005).

The White Ash is placed in the Resource category here, but it has value also as an Ornamental and is often planted in parks and residential neighbourhoods. The tree is good for green spaces that call for a big free-standing specimen. W.T. Macoun, former Dominion Horticulturist, wrote in 1925 that "The tree is shapely, the foliage attractive in appearance throughout the growing season, and in the autumn has a purplish tint, which is very pleasing."

STRONG, SHOCK-ABSORBING WOOD IS GOOD FOR HOCKEY STICKS

The largest of all the ash trees, the White Ash is native to most mixed and deciduous forests in eastern North America. It is highly valued as a hardwood species, along with others such as White Oak, White Pine, Sugar Maple and Yellow Birch. The tree needs fertile soil and avoids moisture and temperature extremes.

Hockey sticks are made from White Ash. The strong, shock-absorbing wood has many other uses in sports equipment manufacturing as well as in the lumber and furniture industries.

Deer and beaver eat White Ash leaves, twigs, and bark. Birds consume the seeds. Bacterial and viral diseases damage leaves, branches, and trunks and the health of infected trees can be worsened by some pollutants.

Many of the single, winged seeds remain on trees long after leaf-fall.

A White Ash tree grows steadily, reaching a height of over 20 m in about 100 years. Its long, oval crown comprises many branches.

Bark on the White Ash, as on other ash species, is narrowly furrowed and grey in colour.

Each vigorous twig has noticeable leaf scars enclosing the base of brown buds.

Upper branches are topped by "brushes" of twigs.

k.gier

Fraxinus pennsylvanica

RED ASH

Compound leaves appear at the same time as flowers.

Found in the Circle, the oldest Red Ash in the Arboretum was planted in 1897. Others are located just north of the poplar area, in the Woodlands and at the southern end.

Ash trees, including Red, White and European Ash, were planted in 1889 in the forest belts along the northern (Carling Avenue) and western (Fisher Avenue) perimeters of the Central Experimental Farm in Ottawa. Among the fastest growing trees, they proved to be successful for their value in timber stands and shelterbelts. Seeds and young trees were shipped to settlers on the prairies for use in shelterbelts.

ONE OF THE MORE COMMON NATIVE ASH TREES

The Red Ash is one of the most commonly found ash trees among those native to central and eastern North America. It grows with oaks, maples and elms in deciduous forests from Nova Scotia to Florida. The tree has high demands for soil fertility, but occurs on sites where water drainage is poor. Its wood is hard, although not as hard as that of White Ash, and the best logs are harvested for furniture making and construction. Landscape architects value Red Ash trees for use along streets and in parks.

When Red Ash trees become big and old, they can play host to cavity-nesting birds and animals. Abundant seed crops will often occur on female trees if male trees grow nearby. This ash is easily transplanted and cultivated, and stump sprouts may replace damaged trees. Some insects, like Ash Borer, and the disease called Ash Yellows may cause serious problems to planted and naturally growing Red Ash trees.

Red Ash in the fall.

Opposite buds (above) sit on top of the flat edge of leaf scars, unlike the White Ash where buds are enclosed. Red Ash buds are brown, while buds of European Ash are black.

Bark is smooth and thin on small trees, becoming coarse and splitting into thick, diamond-shaped, corky scales as the tree matures.

Wind-pollinated female flowers produce numerous winged seeds that gradually disperse in late fall and winter.

While ash trees may be easy to spot, differences between species are harder to see. For differences between male and female flowers, refer to European Ash.

The Red Ash is a tall, fast-growing tree with a broad, oval-shaped crown. Branches are upright and arching with many stiff twigs.

k.gier

Tilia americana
BASSWOOD

Alternately arranged, heart-shaped leaves are about 10 to 15 cm long, dark green above and whitish underneath.

Clusters of fragrant, light yellow flowers grow on most peripheral twigs.

The Basswood's many small clusters of creamy yellow, fragrant flowers typically draw hordes of bees, whose humming around this tree has given it the name of "the humming tree."

"Hardly a finer honey exists than that produced from Basswood flowers; gourmets regard its slightly minty flavour as exquisite." (Eastman, 1992)

A BROAD, ROUND CROWN AND LARGE LEAVES

A Basswood grows quickly into a beautiful big tree that produces dense shade from its broad, rounded crown and large leaves. It tolerates compacted soils and air pollution, which makes it very useful for spacious landscapes in urban settings. A wide-spreading Basswood can be seen at the southern end of the old Windbreak towards Dow's Lake.

Also known as American Linden, Whitewood and Lime Trees, Basswood trees are native to eastern North American forests where they accompany oaks and maples. They grow best in fine-textured soils where there are no extremely wet or dry conditions. Basswood trees often grow in ravines and along creeks. Their leaves are rich in minerals that nourish and replenish the soil. "They are living, breathing, non-polluting fertilizer factories." (Blouin, 2001)

The wood of these trees is soft, light and tough, and is used commercially to make boxes. It is also an easy wood for carvers and sculptors. In mid-summer, many pollinating insects besides bees feed at the Basswood blooms and birds and small rodents eat the nuts later in the season. Basswood is not particularly attractive to pests, although aphids, Japanese beetles, leafminers and borers can damage the leaves and trunks.

A Basswood tree is relatively large and may have one or more stems. Numerous suckers come out from the base.

Small nuts are attached to whitish-green papery bracts. Large crops of nuts are shed in early fall.

Thick, grey-brown bark has long, flat-topped ridges.

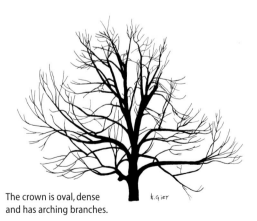

k.Gier

The crown is oval, dense and has arching branches.

Fagus grandifolia
AMERICAN BEECH

Its twigs show a zigzag pattern with thin, pointed leathery leaves at each turning point. Leaves turn a copper-bronze colour in the fall and may stay on the tree through the winter.

In open areas, such as at the southern end of the Arboretum, the tree can branch out very low down and form a large crown of wide-spreading branches.

The tree's fruit is a shiny brown triangular nut enclosed in a spiky husk; ripe nuts fall off in September.

The only native beech in North America, the American Beech was once abundant in the Ottawa area. It is native to the hardwood regions of Canada stretching from Cape Breton Island, Nova Scotia to Georgian Bay, Ontario. American Beech trees of various ages can be found in the Woodlands area of the Arboretum as well as at the southern end.

With proper pruning when young, the American Beech can "form a more beautiful tree than most others," wrote A.R. Buckley, former Curator of the Arboretum. To see how well it can be pruned, visit the Farm's hedge collection in the Campus area, where there is a giant American Beech hedge planted in the early 1900s.

LOVE LETTERS ON THE BARK

Thin tablets of beech wood were once used as writing material. Thus, many words for "book" in eastern European languages are derived from "beech". Perhaps this ancient use finds an echo in the often-found carvings of love notes on the smooth bark of beech trees. Unfortunately, this practice can allow disease to enter and damage a tree.

The American Beech is seldom seen lining the streets of big cities, but is frequently planted as a shade tree in urban parks and recreational areas. Its shallow, wide-spreading roots need moisture near the surface and good drainage. Extremely wet or dry conditions can threaten its growth.

Popular as firewood because of the high heat it generates, the wood of American Beech trees is now also used for flooring, furniture, veneer and plywood. Many birds and animals feed on the fatty beech nuts, which are rich in protein and calcium. No major pest problems have been reported for this tree in the Arboretum.

When it grows naturally in a close stand, as in the Woodlands area of the Arboretum, the American Beech has a straight, erect trunk with branches only beginning to appear at a good height.

It is readily identified by its thin, smooth, grey bark. (While this may invite the markings of amorous couples and others, such carvings can cause disease.)

Flowers bloom just after the leaves have come out. Male (pollen) flowers occur in rounded heads; female flowers in spikes of two to four.

Betula papyrifera
PAPER BIRCH

"The full beauty of white-barked trees is displayed better during spring, summer and fall against the verdure of our lawns, and yet a White Birch against the light blue winter's sky can stand out brilliantly."
A.R. BUCKLEY, FORMER CURATOR OF THE ARBORETUM, 1964

Simple alternate leaves are diamond or triangle shaped.

The white trunks and transparent crowns of Paper Birch trees, also known as White Birch and Canoe Birch, decorate many parks and residential areas. There is no mature Paper Birch in the Arboretum (spring 2007), but among promising young trees is one in the southern crab apple area near the bridge.

The value of the Paper Birch as a fast-growing resource tree was proven in the experimental forest belts at the Farm. Planted in 1888, in 22 years it became second in height and diameter, among deciduous trees, to the American Elm. It was recommended to farmers for use in mixed stands of deciduous trees and conifers for both shelter and timber.

SASKATCHEWAN'S OFFICIAL TREE
The Paper Birch grows in all Canadian provinces and territories, and is the official tree of Saskatchewan. It tolerates sandy and clay soils. Growing on dry rocky outcrops and wet lowlands near the northern timberline, and on the edge of prairie land, the best growth, however, occurs on deep fertile soils away from climatic extremes.

MANY USES, FROM BIRCH BARK CANOES TO BEER
First Nations people used the bark of Paper Birch for canoes, the sap for sugar, the roots for dyes and many parts of the tree for medicine. The sap can also be used to make beer, wine and vinegar. The wood of the Paper Birch is hard and is used, for example, as a veneer in furniture-making and for flooring, toothpicks and popsicle sticks.

Their crowns are compact and transparent. Twigs are thin and are not pendulous on this species.

k.gier

Male and female flowers are gathered in separate catkins, but grow on the same tree. Male catkins, hanging down, release pollen in spring. Upright female catkins disperse small, two-winged seeds in late summer.

Bark changes colour from dark reddish-brown to chalk white during the first 5 to 10 years.

Snowshoe hare, deer, and moose browse young birch in forests all year round. Some birds eat the buds and catkins in winter. Many diseases and pests attack this birch, the most dangerous being the Bronze Birch Borer, a beetle that can kill healthy, mature trees in one to two years. The Paper Birch is also sensitive to pollution.

fyi *Paper Birch trees grow quickly, reaching their maximum height in about 30 years. Trees are often multi-stemmed and do not have large limbs.*

Betula alleghaniensis
YELLOW BIRCH

"Ah, such fleeting beauty: by 60 a birch is elderly, and by 100 positively Methuselan." MARJORIE HARRIS, 2003

Meet Methuselah in the Arboretum; a Yellow Birch, planted in 1890 just north of Building 72. With its compact form and contorted branches, it looks at home among the crab apples. A few younger Yellow Birch trees can be found among the oaks at the southern end of the Arboretum.

First planted in the Farm's forest belt in 1889, Yellow Birches became well established. Also known as Swamp Birch, saplings were dug up in 1894 from a swamp near the Farm and these, too, did well. They also proved to make a good, tall hedge at the Farm.

Unlike other birches, the Yellow Birch is slow growing. It is found in forests with hemlock, beech, Sugar Maple and Red Spruce trees. Growth is best on moist and fertile soils along river valleys and on uplands. This birch grows well in parks, recreational green space and on street lawns, as long as it does not face prolonged drought.

Simple, alternate leaves are oval and elongated, an unusual feature for birch trees. Upright seed clusters are the largest of all native birches.

Male and female flowers are gathered in separate catkins, but grow on the same tree. Male catkins elongate before the release of pollen in spring. Upright female catkins start to disperse small winged seeds in late summer.

VALUABLE HARDWOOD FOR FINE FURNITURE

The longest-living and largest native birch in North America, Yellow Birch is prized for its hardwood lumber. The wood, which can be highly polished, is used for fine furniture and cabinet-making.

Unfortunately, many diseases and pests attack this birch, the most dangerous of which are dieback and Bronze Birch Borer. Animals dine on Yellow Birch twigs, buds, leaves, and young bark, and some birds eat both buds and catkins.

This impressive old Yellow Birch in the Arboretum, planted in an open area, has not grown large and tall.

Distinctive bark is thin, yellow-bronze and smooth. Mature trees display small horizontal curls of outer bark.

fyi *The Yellow Birch (le bouleau jaune) is the provincial tree of Quebec.*

The crown usually consists of long upright branches, often beginning close to the ground. This young birch in the drawing is competing for space with oaks.

k.gier

Thuja occidentalis
EASTERN WHITE CEDAR

Twigs are thin and very flexible. They end in flat shoots with flat scaly leaves, which are dark green on top and a lighter green underneath.

Male and female cones are solitary, but grow in groups on the tips of twigs of the same tree. Ripe female cones open in the fall and release small two-winged seeds.

The Eastern White Cedar is a very popular ornamental tree, suitable for large and small properties, and easy to grow and transplant. Many varieties have been cultivated for use in landscaping. According to *The Living Collection of the Dominion Arboretum* (Douglas, 2005), there were 45 varieties of Eastern White Cedar in the Arboretum in 2005.

Eastern White Cedars are also popular for hedges. By 1894 such hedges stretched more than a mile along the boundaries of the Central Experimental Farm, as well as near buildings and in the experimental hedge collection.

RENOWNED FOR ITS RESISTANCE TO DECAY

The Eastern White Cedar is included here in the Resource category because of the value of its dry wood in resisting decay from moist soil or air. Although knotty, the wood is extensively used for fence posts, shingles, telephone poles and railroad ties. First Nations people used it for the frames and ribs of birchbark canoes, because it doesn't warp or shrink.

The natural habitat for Eastern White Cedars is the North American boreal forest from the Atlantic coast to the prairies. They can reach the height of fir, hemlock, and spruce trees, but only at moist sites in rich, fertile soils. Forest fires will easily kill Eastern White Cedar trees, but they return much later, when the forest has been restored by pioneer pine or birch stands.

Eastern White Cedar trees provide good shelter for birds and animals, and are a favourite winter food of deer. The dense crown casts a cooling shade in summer and protects against harsh winds. In urban environments, the trees do not face any serious pests or diseases and are resistant to pollution, but can be damaged by heavy salt spray.

The crowns of Eastern White Cedars are dense and can be conical or narrow, as on the tree in the foreground of the photo.

On large trunks, the bark is thin with long, narrow strips.

When arching, lower branches touch the ground, as in this young 'Pyramidalis' variety, they may become rooted and produce new trees.

Populus deltoides
EASTERN COTTONWOOD

The majestic Eastern Cottonwood in the photo can be seen from the Southern Lookout in a group of tall poplars, all planted around 1901. The yellowy-white tufts of cottonlike seeds which give this tree its name, float in the breeze early in summer, covering the grass and piling up along the path by the tree. In some public places, male trees are preferred, to avoid this cloud of fluff.

There are about 40 species of poplar in the world and thousands of varieties or hybrids. In 2005, *The Living Collection of the Dominion Arboretum* (Douglas, 2005) lists 33 species and varieties.

FAST GROWING WITH SPREADING ROOTS

The Eastern Cottonwood is native to eastern North America excluding northern and coastal areas. It is a pioneer tree, among the first to come back to disturbed sites, where it establishes itself in pure stands. Other types of tree, such as elm, oak, and ash, invade later and replace aging poplars. Moist, sandy bottomlands and stream banks are the natural habitats for this tree, but plantations do occur elsewhere. The wood of the Eastern Cottonwood is light and soft, with commercial value as lumber, veneer, plywood, particleboard and pulpwood.

While it is an easy tree to grow, it may spread and its shallow, spreading root system can buckle sidewalks and damage sewers. Rural and urban developers use this tree for quick soil stabilization and site reclamation. Because of its fast growth and spreading roots it is also useful for erosion control and for shelterbelts and windbreaks.

The leaves and buds of the Eastern Cottonwood give off a sweet smell when crushed. Its branches and cavities offer good

Female trees regularly produce cotton-like masses of seeds in early summer (top). Leaves are triangular, hence the Latin designation *deltoides*.

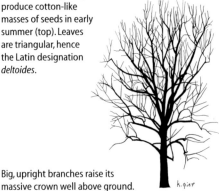

Big, upright branches raise its massive crown well above ground.

k.gier

Eastern Cottonwoods are the fastest growing native trees in North America, becoming large trees, up to 30 m high, in less than 40 years. This one was planted in the Arboretum in 1901, far exceeding an average life span of 50 to 70 years for the species.

Bark on young trees is smooth. As trees mature, it becomes very thick and coarse, light grey in colour.

Tiny male and female flowers, gathered in catkins, grow on separate trees. Wind and flowing water disperse short-living seeds over large areas.

places for birds to build nests. Young trees provide nutritious browsing for deer, beavers and rabbits. Dozens of diseases and insects damage or kill trees, but sprouts or suckers often come back from stumps or roots.

Ulmus americana
AMERICAN ELM

Alternately-arranged leaves, like those of other elms, have an asymmetric base and forked veins.

Large branches start well above the ground and grow upright. Many thin branches make long, wide arches.

k.gier

The American Elm has a distinctive vase or umbrella shape, with branches that reach upwards and outwards in a graceful arching pattern. Its beauty and elegance have made it a favourite among native trees. American Elms are tall, able to provide a high canopy over city avenues and boulevards. At the Central Experimental Farm, since 1888, they have been planted along the National Capital Commission Driveway, formerly called Elm Avenue.

A DEVASTATING DISEASE FOR A GRACEFUL, ELEGANT TREE

American Elms survive infections and infestations of many fungi and insects, but do not withstand attacks of the Dutch Elm Disease (DED) fungus. First isolated in the Netherlands around 1920, DED proved to be devastating in North America. The first outbreak in Canada was discovered in 1944.

The American Elm is a native tree of eastern North America. Also known as White Elm and Water Elm, its range is vast, but its presence in mixed deciduous forests has been drastically reduced by DED. It grows on plains and along watercourses with Red and Sugar Maples, White and Red Oaks. The American Elm's hard wood, nearly impossible to split, is scarce and highly valued.

Easily transplanted, fast-growing, tolerant of limb and root pruning, and surviving in a variety of soils, the American Elm and its cultivars remain popular ornamental trees in North America, despite Dutch Elm Disease. Because the vulnerability of American Elms to disease increases with age, there are fewer and fewer old specimens around. Younger ones, such as those of the disease-resistant 'American Liberty' cultivar, can be seen in the Arboretum beside the southern paths.

The American Elm grows rapidly when young. It builds a large, fine-textured crown, which is widest at the top.

The bark is coarse with deep furrows and scaly, crossing ridges.

Seeds develop quickly, becoming ripe before leaves are fully developed.

Clusters of small flowers of both sexes appear before the leaves. Twigs are thin and the topmost bud is often smaller than other buds.

fyi *A single tree disseminates millions of seeds every summer, which start to grow immediately after they fall on moist ground.*

Abies balsamea
BALSAM FIR

Male and female cones appear on the same tree in early summer. Seed-bearing cones are upright and easy to see at the top of branches in mid summer. Mature cones release small winged seeds in the fall.

Dark green needles grow flat on twigs and remain for a few years. A distinguishing feature is the clean snap of the needles when bent.

In the woods, the attractive conical shape and deep green, glossy foliage of the Balsam Fir provide a striking contrast to a background of fall hardwoods. Its shape and foliage have made the Balsam Fir a popular Christmas tree, grown in plantations for that purpose. Two tall, mature Balsam Fir trees grow side by side in the centre of the Circle area at the Arboretum.

The Balsam Fir is also known for its production of Canada Balsam, a pleasant-smelling resin, that gathers on the bark under blisters. This resin has had various industrial, medicinal and nutritional uses, from cementing lenses on microscopes to an emergency, nutritious food in the forest. With some sweetening, it was once sold as a candy.

COMMON IN CANADIAN FORESTS, VALUABLE AT CHRISTMAS TIME

Balsam Fir, the official tree of New Brunswick, is one of the most common trees in the boreal forest east of the Rocky Mountains. It often outnumbers spruce and pine trees in the evergreen woods of eastern regions and, across the continent, it forms dense lower layers in mixed forests. Balsam Fir tolerates a wide range of soil moisture, but will not grow on dry, sandy or rocky sites. Its light and soft wood is good for pulp but in less demand for lumber. Its highest economic value is at Christmas time.

Balsam Fir buds and seeds feed birds and small animals. Lower branches and young trees are winter food for deer and moose. Dense crowns on Balsam Fir trees provide shelter for wildlife from summer heat and winter cold. Trees are prone to damage by wind, which can uproot them and break rotting trunks. The Balsam Fir suffers from many dangerous pests and root-rot diseases. Spruce Budworm moths, which prefer firs to spruces, periodically kill all mature fir trees on thousands of acres.

Balsam Fir trees grow rapidly in sunny situations, forming dense, narrow crowns with slightly uplifted branches.

Bark is thin on both young and mature Balsam Firs. Numerous, horizontal pitch blisters containing sap (Canada Balsam) are close to the outer surface.

Male cones appear on the edges of lower branches.

Celtis occidentalis

COMMON HACKBERRY

Alternate leaves, with sharp tips and asymmetrical bases, are up to 10 cm long. The Common Hackberry produces an abundant crop of berries (or drupes), which are small and vary in colour from orange to red, purple or black.

The Common Hackberry is a moderately tall tree with a life span of about 100 years. It has a massive trunk at the base and big wide branches.

k.gier

Related to the elm, the Common Hackberry was thought to be a possible successor to the American Elm, if that species ever became extinct due to Dutch Elm Disease. The Common Hackberry is immune to the disease, is very tolerant of the urban environment, and is also useful for erosion control. Although it cannot claim the majesty and beauty of the elm, the tree has nevertheless proved a useful stand-in on city streets.

Young Common Hackberries, along with American Elms, are beside the path leading to the south of the Arboretum, beyond the group of catalpas. Old Common Hackberry specimens are found in the Circle area.

BOIS INCONNU

"Early French settlers called it 'bois inconnu' — loosely translated as the unidentifiable tree". (Blouin, 2001) *Celtis* trees are known as nettle-trees in Europe because their leaves resemble those of nettles, while *Celtis occidentalis* is called Sugarberry in England because of its sweet fruit.

A native of eastern North America, the Common Hackberry plays a minor part in deciduous forests. It will survive spring floods and summer droughts, although the best growth occurs in deep, fertile soils. The timber of mature Common Hackberry trees is of poor quality.

A FAVOURITE WITH THE BIRDS

The sweet fruits of the Common Hackberry are a good winter food source for many bird species. Deer browse on the leaves of young trees. Although many insects and diseases can be found on the leaves, twigs, branches and trunk, damage is usually only cosmetic and does not destroy the tree.

Corky bark has a distinct ornamental pattern. Small green-yellow flowers, gathered in clusters, appear just before new leaves emerge. Twigs never grow straight and do not have terminal buds.

Tsuga canadensis
EASTERN HEMLOCK

Because of the Eastern Hemlock's dense crown and thick foliage, it casts one of the darkest shades of any evergreen. Such shade can be experienced beneath the handsome Eastern Hemlocks, planted in 1947, in the collection of evergreens in the southern section of the Circle area. An old specimen with a more ragged appearance can be seen near the entrance to the Arboretum.

A GIANT FROM A TINY CONE

Eastern Hemlocks occur naturally in mixed forests throughout north-eastern North America. They are found only in very old forests, where there have been no fires for hundreds of years. Even light forest fires will kill them, regardless of their size. White Pine, maples, beech, and Yellow and Paper Birches shelter young hemlocks and give them a chance to become forest giants. The species tolerates shade, has a high demand for nutrients, and never grows well on poor, dry or wet soils.

Twigs are hairy and needles appear to be arranged in two rows. Male and female cones appear in the spring on the same tree, but at different positions. Female cones grow on the tips of twigs, male ones are hidden inside the crown.

Eastern Hemlocks grow into large trees. They are giants in the forest, and yet have tiny cones, distinguishing them from spruce and fir trees. They are durable in parks, as long as they are not exposed to salt spray.

First Nations people have traditionally brewed tea from the young needles of the Eastern Hemlock. (The suicide potion of Socrates came from an entirely different hemlock plant.) Although the wood of the Eastern Hemlock is light, breakable and coarse-grained, it has multiple uses in wood and construction industries.

The dense crowns of Eastern Hemlocks provide protection for many birds, which also feed on the cones. Twigs of small Eastern Hemlocks provide food for deer and snowshoe hares in winter. Many diseases and insects infect these trees, but most damage is caused by drought, soil compaction and street salt spray.

Many thin horizontal branches descend to the ground.

Eastern Hemlock grows slowly, taking decades to exceed 10 m in height. This old specimen is at the entrance to the Arboretum.

Brown-grey bark has a purple hue under broken, corky scales.

Seeds are released from mature cones, gradually over a few months in the fall.

The crown is conical. The leading shoot is at a slant.

Ostrya virginiana
IRONWOOD

Alternately-arranged, simple leaves often have forks on veins similar to those on elm leaves. Elongated clusters of tiny female flowers appear on the ends of peripheral twigs when leaves are completely open.

This species, first planted in the Arboretum in 1898, is also known as American Hop Hornbean, because the pale yellow sacs that contain seeds resemble hops. The common name, Ironwood, comes from its very hard, strong, heavy wood.

THRIVES IN DEEP SHADE

Able to grow in deep shade, Ironwood is an understorey tree in the Woodlands area of the Arboretum. At the same time, its small stature and broad, pyramidal shape make it attractive on its own. Individual Ironwood trees can be seen near the two lookouts in the Arboretum.

WILL FLOURISH ALMOST ANYWHERE

Ironwood trees are common in the old, mixed and deciduous forests of eastern North America. They do not grow to the same size as maple, beech, or basswood trees, but exceed the height of large shrubs. Ironwood trees avoid wet or flooded bottoms of river valleys but an individual Ironwood "has the admirable ability to flourish almost anywhere. It's rather like one of those people who keeps popping up in the most unexpected places." (Harris, 2003)

Male catkins, fall seeds and winter buds provide food for forest birds and animals. The tree does not suffer from disease or pests and is cold-hardy. Because of its small size it requires no pruning or trimming in park settings, but it will not tolerate salt damage. Although the wood is hard and strong, the tree is small. Good logs for sawing are rare.

Each female flower in the cluster develops a leafy sac containing one small seed.

Bark is thin throughout the life of a tree, with small, rectangular flakes on mature trees.

Male flower catkins are visible long before pollination occurs in early summer.

Ironwood trees grow rapidly when young, like this one near the Eastern Lookout. They grow slowly when mature.

The narrow, sharp pointed crown flattens with age, although branches continue to be upright.

k.gier

Larix laricina
TAMARACK

Like other larch trees, the Tamarack has two distinct patterns of needles on the same branch: single-spaced on long shoots and in tufts on short shoots. The soft needles turn yellow before falling in autumn.

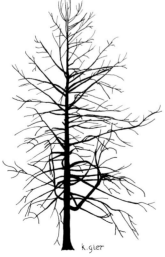

Both young and mature trees have transparent, narrow crowns with slightly upright branches.

k.gier

The Tamarack is also known as American Larch, Eastern Larch and Hackmatack. It occurs in the northern boreal forest in every province and territory of Canada, as well as in Alaska, and is the only native larch in eastern Canada.

Pure stands of Tamarack occur in bogs and wetlands. The trees also grow along with Black or White Spruce, fir and alders on moist sites. Vigorous berry-producing shrubs often thrive beneath a sparse Tamarack canopy. Tamaracks provide an abundant seed crop for birds and small animals at least once every five years.

Mature Tamarack trees grow at the Arboretum at the south end of the small island. A beautiful young Tamarack near the Eastern Lookout is trying a drier location. In the early years, Tamarack was tested at the Experimental Farms in Western Canada for use in a windbreak or shelterbelt and was recommended for western conditions.

HARDY AND HEALTHY

Because of its great hardiness in cold climates, the Tamarack is planted in parks and along streets in towns where few trees can survive the cold. It does not tolerate shade at any age; but in parks it is a healthy tree with a light, graceful appearance.

As with all larches, its wood is hard and durable and is now valued mainly in the pulpwood industry. Because it is strong and does not rot easily, Tamarack wood was important in the building of sailing ships, telephone poles and railroad ties. "The last spike was likely driven into a tamarack tie." (Blouin, 2001)

Tamarack trees, like this young one near the Eastern Lookout to Dow's Lake, grow fast only for a few decades.

Bark becomes coarse and corky on old Tamaracks , yet gives no fire protection to the tree.

fyi *Tamarack is the only native larch in eastern Canada.*

Female cones are smaller than those on any other species of larch in the Arboretum. They consist of less than 10 small seed-scales.

Acer rubrum
RED MAPLE

First planted in 1890, large Red Maples can be seen in the maple section of the Arboretum. Although it is a valuable resource tree, the Red Maple also makes a fine ornamental because there is red on the tree all year round. In spring, tiny red flowers appear long before any leaves and before the flowering of most other trees.

SPECTACULAR COLOUR
In summer, the seeds and stems of its leaves are red. Spectacular red foliage celebrates the fall season while red buds and twigs adorn the winter tree.

The Red Maple occurs naturally in eastern North America. It can tolerate a wide range of conditions, from swamps to rocky uplands to urban landscapes, but it is somewhat susceptible to wind damage. The wood is marketed as "soft maple." Not as heavy and strong as Sugar Maple, a "hard maple," it nevertheless can be used to produce fine furniture and cabinets. It is commonly used today as pulpwood.

FOOD FOR WILDLIFE
The Red Maple produces lots of seeds almost every year, feeding many birds and animals. Twigs and buds of young trees are a good food source for deer and elk. Insects can cause damage, but are not a serious threat.

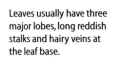

Leaves usually have three major lobes, long reddish stalks and hairy veins at the leaf base.

Red, winged seeds hang in clusters; twigs are reddish.

Clusters of female and male flowers appear on different branches of the same tree before leaves come out.

k.gier

The tree is open and medium-sized, rather than thick and massive.

Ash-grey bark is smooth on young trees; rough and flaky when mature.

Acer saccharinum
SILVER MAPLE

fyi *Note the similarity in Latin name, meaning sweet or sugary, to the Sugar Maple or Acer saccharum. Sap of the Silver Maple has just half the sugar content of the Sugar Maple.*

A fast growing tree, the Silver Maple becomes large in less then 50 years. It has a few massive upright branches.

k.gier

Among the first trees planted at the Farm, Silver Maples soon became prominent features of the Arboretum. The former Dominion Horticulturist, W.T. Macoun, in 1909 recommended the Silver Maple as one of the best ornamental deciduous trees hardy in Ottawa, with its "clean, clear cut, green leaves, handsome form, delicately and highly tinted leaves in autumn."

THE GRACEFUL MAPLE
The specimen in the photo stands beside the southward path in the maple section, where other Silver Maples can be found. Its graceful branches almost touch the ground, as they do on the tree whose trunk is shown in the photo. That one is among the ash trees at the bottom of the hill in the southern section. Visitors to the Ornamental Gardens can see a fine old variety of Silver Maple by the iris and daylily beds.

MOISTURE-LOVING
The Silver Maple is widespread through central and eastern North America. It is moisture-loving, and grows largest on bottomland, near streams or on sites where water is slow to drain. It produces the most wood when it grows on fine textured soils. The wood is heavy but not strong and is valued by lumber producers and furniture makers where strength is not required.

LOVED BY ANIMALS AND BIRDS
The tree's seed crop is an important food source for many birds and animals. Its spacious crown provides excellent nesting sites and the trunks of the Silver Maple are often hollow, providing appealing dens for animals, birds and children.

Silver Maple wood is brittle. Strong wind or heavy ice may split or break its big branches.

On the large trunk of mature trees, bark is light grey with coarse, loose flakes.

Despite its size, sunlight penetrates through the crown of the Silver Maple. "It is the most graceful of all the maples, the deeply cut leaves giving it a lighter look than the others." (W.T. Macoun)

Opposite, simple leaves are deeply cut into three to five lobes.

Clusters of small greenish-yellow flowers produce numerous winged seeds (or samaras). These may be up to 5 cm long, larger than those of other maples.

Acer saccharum

SUGAR MAPLE

"The best all round ornamental tree hardy at Ottawa."

Dark green leaves have smooth edges and usually have five lobes. In the fall, leaves are orange and yellow.

Twigs and thin branches grow upright and survive in inner parts of crown for years.

k.gier

So said the former Dominion Horticulturist, W.T. Macoun, in his annual report of 1925. The Sugar Maple "gives the impression of strength and fitness for planting … as single specimens or groups on the lawn." Beautiful large specimens can be found in the maple section of the Arboretum and also past the oaks at the southern end.

CANADIANS AND THE SUGAR MAPLE

Canadians, especially those who live east of Manitoba, have great affection for the Sugar Maple. Tapping the sweet sap of the tree in the sugar bush is a Canadian tradition. Sugar Maple (*Acer saccharum*) and the Silver Maple (*Acer saccharinum*) derive their Latin names from the word meaning sweet or sugary. The sap of the Sugar Maple has twice the sugar content of the Silver Maple.

The Sugar Maple, found from the Maritimes to the Ontario-Manitoba border, is an important Canadian symbol. The maple leaf on the Canadian flag is a stylized version of all native maples, but it most closely resembles the Sugar Maple leaf.

ONE OF THE MOST POPULAR HARDWOODS

Known as "hard maple" on the lumber market, the hardwood of the Sugar Maple is one of the most popular in North America, highly valued for furniture, flooring and a whole range of other uses.

After a few decades of growth in sunny spots, the Sugar Maple becomes a prodigious seed producer. The tree is also very tolerant of shade. Big trees grow in old deciduous forests in deep fertile soils.

(above) A large tree, the Sugar Maple slowly develops a massive trunk and dense crown, continuing to grow vigorously for over 100 years.

(left) Seeds hang down in clusters, ripening in late summer. Keys (or samaras) are in U-shaped pairs.

As it matures, smooth bark becomes coarse with loose irregular ridges and plates.

The Sugar Maple, along with its various cultivars, is a popular choice in rural and suburban landscaping. It is resistant to pests and diseases, but does less well downtown, where it is affected by street pollutants, soil compaction and drought.

Pinus banksiana

JACK PINE

Pairs of short needles grow on thin, upright shoots.

I f you see some rather scraggly evergreens that vary in shape, you may be looking at Jack Pines. A tall one, planted in 1921, stands in the centre of the Circle area of the Arboretum. It has the irregular branch pattern that has made the Jack Pine a feature of the Canadian forest. This tree can add a wild look to an ornamental landscape. In cold climates, Jack Pines and some shrub-like cultivars are used in urban settings for their hardiness.

Also known as Scrub Pine, Jack Pine was once considered a weed tree by the forest industry. Its timber is now used for pulpwood and lowgrade lumber. The wood is weak, resinous and coarse textured, and does not last long in humid environments.

TIGHTLY SEALED CONES
LAST FOR YEARS

Jack Pines are also recognized by their curved cones, which are sealed tight with resin and remain on a tree for several years. The heat of a forest fire will open the cone and release the seeds, allowing the Jack Pine to begin a new forest. It is the only tree to come back when frequent fires occur. It will dominate on the poorest soils, but is easily overtaken by spruce, fir or aspen on fertile sites.

A North American tree, the Jack Pine grows in most of the eastern and central boreal forest. It provides little food but good shelter for birds and animals. The breeding habitat for the rare Kirtland's Warbler is young Jack Pine woods. It is a healthy tree in parks, but root-rot fungi and street pollutants can make the Jack Pine's short life span even shorter. Pruning of lower branches may be needed on partially shaded trees.

Crowns of both young and mature trees are transparent and scrubby. Branches grow in all directions.

Orange-yellow male and reddish female cones appear on new growth in early summer.

The Jack Pine is a fast-growing and relatively short-lived tree that reaches its maximum height in 50 to 60 years.

The bark is coarse with small irregular flakes that do not form ridges and furrows.

Winged seeds are sealed inside stalkless, curved cones and remain viable on trees for several years.

fyi *The name* banksiana *honours Sir Joseph Banks, botanist and former Director of the Royal Botanic Gardens, Kew, in London, England, who explored the east coast of Canada in the late 1760s with Captain James Cook.*

Excessive heat from fire or sun is needed to open the cone scales.

Pinus resinosa
RED PINE

The Red Pine is one of the fastest growing pines in the Ottawa area. It is native to northeastern North America. First planted in the Arboretum in 1889, the oldest remaining Red Pine dates from 1895 and can be found in the Circle. Young Red Pines form a new windbreak along the Rideau Canal between Dow's Lake and Hartwell Locks while Red Pines of various ages can be found in the Campus area of the Farm.

Red Pines can live several hundred years and can reach a height of 35 m with a trunk of up to 1.5 m in diameter. They are able to grow on exposed sites and withstand strong winds because of a root system which can extend 10 m and penetrate up to 4 m below the ground.

Red Pine wood, heavier than that of White Pine, is an excellent structural timber and has been used for telephone poles, piles, window frames and doors. It is often used in reforestation, parks and windbreaks, although it tends not to do well in the smoke and dust of cities. Red Pine will often dominate in the forest after fires.

LOW-MAINTENANCE CHOICE
The Red Pine provides shelter, nesting sites and food for many species of birds and animals. No major pest problems have been recorded in the Arboretum and only minor trimming or pruning has been required.

Red Pine has thick dark green needles in clusters of two and up to 16 cm long. The needles are brittle and break when bent.

Purple male flowers (above) are found in groups around the base of new shoots; red female flowers (top) are at the tips of new shoots; both occur on the same tree.

Mature trees have a rounded crown with symmetrical whorls of big branches.

Mature seeds are released in the early fall from light brown cones (above), which stay open on the tree until spring.

Soft reddish-brown bark is covered with thin, flaky scales.

Pinus strobus
EASTERN WHITE PINE

"The Eastern White Pine is better known as a timber tree than as one for ornamental purposes, but when it has sufficient space for the side branches to develop well it becomes one of the most graceful evergreens. Its leaves, which are of a lively green, do not become as dull in winter as some others." W.T. MACOUN, FORMER DOMINION HORTICULTURIST, 1924

The Eastern White Pine is the provincial tree of Ontario. It is also known as Weymouth Pine, after Lord Weymouth of Wiltshire, England, who planted the tree on his estate in the 18th century.

A close relative of the Eastern White Pine is the Western White Pine *(Pinus monticola)* and fine old specimens of each of these species can be found and compared close together inside the Circle near the Eastern Lookout. The oldest Eastern White Pine is close to the Arboretum entrance.

THE TALLEST TREE IN EASTERN CANADA

The Eastern White Pine is the tallest tree in eastern Canada. In mixed forests of eastern North America, it grows in light soils as long as sites are not extremely dry. Young trees tolerate shade and will survive for decades under an open forest canopy. The Western White Pine is a mountain dweller scattered along river valleys from British Columbia to California, needing full sun to become a large healthy tree.

Bytown, which was to become Ottawa, was founded 150 years ago on the huge supply of white pine lumber. The tall cylindrical trunks of the Eastern White Pine and its light, almost non-resinous wood were highly valued by shipbuilders in the nineteenth century. The wood has high commercial value today for

continued...

Needles of the Eastern (above) and Western (top and left) White Pines differ in size, but both are soft, long and come in bundles of five.

Cones of the two species differ in size but, as with needles, the difference is not always obvious. The young cone is from a Western White Pine, the old one from an Eastern White Pine.

Western White Pine, *Pinus monticola*

Pinus strobus
EASTERN WHITE PINE

Continued from page 156

building and furniture-making, as does that of the Western White Pine. Both species can be found in large urban parks where exposure to air and street pollutants is limited.

Small animals and birds feed on the needles and seeds. Porcupines eat inner bark in winter and may seriously damage top parts of a tree. Flat tops of old trees are used by big birds for nesting. Major problems are White Pine Blister Rust which kills needles, root rot and weevils which eat terminal buds.

On thin branches and young trees, the bark of Eastern and Western White Pines is greenish-grey and smooth; on mature trees it is dark grey-brown and rough. (Photo is of Eastern White Pine.)

Both Eastern and Western White Pines are very large trees living hundreds of years. The most obvious difference between the two species lies in their shape. The Eastern White Pine (above) is asymmetrical, whereas the Western White Pine (opposite) is narrower and more symmetrical.

Populus balsamifera
BALSAM POPLAR

Simple, alternate leaves are leathery, dark green on top and pale underneath. Fragrant, resinous buds (below) are noticeable on tips of reddish-brown twigs. Big male and female catkins grow on different trees, but both appear early in spring before leaves come out.

Growing from coast to coast, the Balsam Poplar is a true native to the northern regions of North America. It occurs in boreal and mixed forests along rivers and creeks on periodically flooded or moist sites. Fertile soils and full sun make the species competitive in harsh climatic conditions.

Balsam Poplars were first planted in the Arboretum in 1890. As with other poplars, their value has been recognized for Resource, Environmental and Ornamental purposes. Found in parts of Canada where other trees are scarce, they have been used for lumber and firewood. They are now used for pulpwood and particleboard. Growing rapidly, these trees have been useful in windbreaks and shelterbelts, and their spreading roots help to stabilize sandy soils.

FRAGRANT BUDS, DARK GREEN LEAVES

The Balsam Poplar is a shapely tree with dark green foliage and a sweet scent of balsam. Because the Balsam Poplar is fast growing and thrives in a variety of soils, it has been used for ornamental purposes in urban landscaping. Drawbacks are its spreading roots which can damage sewers and water systems, and its messy seeds. A fine specimen can be seen at the southern end of the Arboretum, on the slope east of the new crab apple collection.

Balsam Poplar twigs are good food all year round for moose, deer, elk, and beaver. Hare and small rodents eat the juicy bark of young trees in winter. Tall mature trees provide nesting sites on branches and in holes of rotten wood. Forest Tent Caterpillar and wood decay fungi are the most dangerous killers of Balsam Poplar trees in forests. Rotten trunks and root suckers are major problems in urban landscaping.

Young trees have smooth grey-green bark which becomes corky and grey later on.

fyi *Balsam Poplar trees grow very fast both in height and trunk diameter.*

Seed capsules contain many small seeds attached to white silky hairs. Seeds are released in early summer and travel long distances by wind or flowing water. They are viable for less than a month after release.

The crown remains narrow with many upright, thin branches.

k.gier

Picea glauca
WHITE SPRUCE

Short needles are pointed, rigid, and rectangular in cross section. Drooping twigs keep foliage up to 7 years.

Mature seed cones are 3-7 cm long, pale brown in colour with diamond-shaped scales.

White Spruce, also known as Canadian Spruce, is found from coast to coast. Its high-quality, tough, and light wood has had a wide range of uses, from the construction industry to the building of rowing skiffs, gliders and musical instruments. It is also a major source of pulpwood. Now the provincial tree of Manitoba, White Spruce was once an important resource for First Nations people. All parts of this tree were used for food (spruce gum), drink (spruce beer), medicine, building, cooking and other purposes.

The White Spruce also makes a fine ornamental tree, stately because of its form and blue-green foliage. Mature specimens can be seen in the Circle area of the Arboretum where there are also dwarf and weeping cultivars. Because of its dense habit, White Spruce is also popular as a Christmas tree.

HUNDREDS OF YEARS TO GROW IN THE NORTH

White Spruce trees take decades to grow in southern Canada and centuries up north. They grow in pure or mixed forests on uplands and river valleys, tolerating a variety of soils, but not poor or sandy ones, preferring moist sites, not overly saturated. They can be up to 30 m high and over 1 m in trunk diameter.

The dense crowns of White Spruce trees provide good shelter for birds and small mammals. Damage to needles and twigs from fungi is common though not lethal. Mites have been reported as a major problem and pest control may be required in hot dry summers. The Spruce Budworm prefers fir trees and does little damage to spruce trees, unless all firs are dead and the population density of budworms is high. Root rot disease can kill young and mature Spruce. This limits their use in shelterbelts and windbreaks.

Winged seeds fall off the cones during the second winter after pollination.

Bark is smooth and thin on younger trees, scaly on older trees.

White Spruce trees have a straight trunk and narrow upper crown. The conical crown is dense, descending almost to the ground. Lower branches grow long, and remain thin at the base.

FRUIT TREES

Some of the trees presented here in the Fruit category may have been planted in the Arboretum for their Ornamental value; the magnificent oaks, or the crab apples with their dazzling rosy blooms. Other trees, like the Black Walnut, with its precious wood, might fit in the Resource category. In this book, however, these are included with the Fruit trees, because they produce edible nuts, fruit or berries (although not necessarily those to be found at the grocery store).

Nuts were, and still are, an essential part of our diet. First Nations people have collected butternuts and black walnuts for centuries. European settlers continued the practice and experimented with more trees. Several European and Asian walnuts were introduced, but only the Japanese Walnut was suited to the eastern Ontario climate.

Left: European Mountain Ash
Top, left to right: Shagbark Hickory,
European Mountain Ash,
'Golden Spice' Pear
Above: Black Walnuts
Right: Crab Apples

Top: European Bird Cherry
Above: European Mountain
Ash variety
Right: Cherry blossoms

Oak acorns do not look like walnuts or pecans but nevertheless they are nuts by botanical definition, and contain nutrients and oil. In the past, English Oak acorns have fed huge herds of pigs all around the European continent. North American oaks belonging to the white oak group also produce sweet acorns which have been used by First Nations people as food, while acorns of the red oak group have a bitter taste and need special treatment before cooking.

Pines do not generally produce a true nut, but peanut-sized seeds called pine nuts are produced by Swiss Stone and Korean Pines. Sweet and oily, they are an important food for mountain dwellers in the European Alps and eastern Asia.

Hazel nuts are a delicious ingredient in many baked goods and ice-creams. The Turkish Hazel is not currently a prized nut producer, but its nuts are good food.

While other apples and sweet cherries may be larger or tastier, crab apple, Black Cherry and White Mulberry trees can produce juicy and excellent fruit for cooking.

FRUIT

Juglans cinerea
BUTTERNUT

fyi Juglans *is Latin for "Jupiter's nut";* cinerea *means "ash coloured", referring to the bark.*

Compound leaves consist of 11 to 19 leaflets with the terminal leaflet always present.

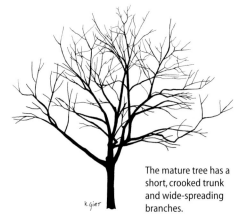

The mature tree has a short, crooked trunk and wide-spreading branches.

k.gier

Butternut trees were first planted in the Arboretum in 1889. The oldest Butternuts in the collection, now about 40 years old, are located by the southern path after it curves around from Prince of Wales Drive past oak, beech and maple trees. The Butternut tree in the photo (opposite) can be seen near Winding Lane off Maple Drive.

SCATTERED AMONG OTHER SPECIES

The Butternut, also known as White Walnut, is native to eastern North America. It is rarely found in pure stands or groves, but tends to be scattered throughout forests of other species such as oak, maple and beech. It thrives beside streams and on fertile sites where its extensive root system helps to control erosion.

Immature nuts and ripe kernels provide food for birds and rodents. Wood borers, nut weevils, husk flies, and bark beetles often damage Butternuts. The major tree killer, however, is the Butternut Canker, a fungus disease (*Sirococcus*). This disease eliminated all originally planted Butternuts. Existing trees have not been proven to be a canker resistant strain.

WOOD USED BY ARTISTS AND ARTISANS

The wood of this species is used by cabinet and furniture makers, and by artists for sculpting and carving. The species produces a sweet, oily nut meat which has been a staple in the diet of First Nations people. W.T. Macoun, former Dominion Horticulturist, wrote in 1925 of the tree as being "a great delight to the young people as the nuts can scarcely be surpassed in flavour."

The mature tree has a wider spread and provides a deeper shade than the Black Walnut.

Nuts are enclosed by a green, fuzzy and sticky husk. The nuts inside are sharply pointed and very hard.

Male catkins (top) and spikes of female flowers (above) occur on the same tree.

You can tell the difference in the bark of the Butternut and the Black Walnut by rubbing your hand over the bark. The diamond-shaped ridges on that of the Butternut are flat; those on the Black Walnut are sharp. Also, the Butternut bark is glossy when wet; the Black Walnut is not.

Prunus serotina
BLACK CHERRY

Elongated clusters of white, bisexual flowers attract many pollinators and nectar collectors in early summer.

Simple, alternate leaves grow on many thin, weeping twigs.

Trees develop a dense, oval crown and a large trunk.

k.gier

Cherry trees are among the most ornamental of plants, famous for their blossoms. The Black Cherry is the largest of the North American cherry species; the only one that ranks as a forest tree. A mature specimen grows just south of the maple area of the Arboretum near the Black Locusts.

Black Cherry trees have white blossoms, dense foliage, long dark leaves and attractive bark. "A good, reliable, medium-sized tree" was how A.R. Buckley, former Curator of the Arboretum, described it. The old Black Cherry in the Arboretum has become irregular and somewhat scraggy, but retains a graceful shape in its major limbs.

Black Cherry trees grow in eastern North American forests and, although similar in size, are always outnumbered by maples, ash, beech and other trees. The Black Cherry grows well in a variety of soils as long as they are moist during most of the growing season. Vigorous stump sprouts may occur on both young and mature trees. Landscape architects avoid using Black Cherry trees on streets because of the litter of their abundant fruit. They are also subject to wind damage and to defoliation by the Forest Tent Caterpillar.

THE BIRD CHERRY
Also known as Wild Cherry, Rum Cherry and Bird Cherry, the Black Cherry provides food for a large number of bird species. Birds eat the cherries and, by their droppings or in regurgitating the pits, start the growth of new trees. Raw fruit of the Black Cherry tree is not palatable to humans, but with sugar, an excellent jelly can be made with them. Young bark and twigs provide food for deer and small mammals when other sources are depleted.

Black Cherry wood is hard and strong,

and considered one of the best woods for fine furniture and cabinet making, second only to that of the Black Walnut. The best logs are harvested in the Appalachian mountains. Their scarcity has made Black Cherry wood very expensive.

Black Cherry trees grow quickly when young and reach over 20 m high on sunny sites.

Black Cherry bark is very different on young and old trees. Initially smooth and thin, it becomes scaly and coarse.

fyi *Fruit of the Black Cherry matures late in the season; hence the Latin name* serotina, *which means "late."*

Malus
CRAB APPLES

Crab apple blossom time at the Farm is a spectacular sight. The magnificent display along Prince of Wales Drive invites the passerby to come in and see the blooming of many more trees throughout the Arboretum. In summer the trees provide attractive shapes and shade, and the fruit are eye-catching in the fall and winter.

A collection of beautiful old crab apples can be found just north of Building 72 near the Arboretum entrance. Another group adorns the area south of the two bridges. A new gallery of crab apple splendour was begun by Brian Douglas, Foreman of the Arboretum and Ornamental Gardens, on the southern slope close to Fletcher Wildlife Garden.

ROSYBLOOMS OF OTTAWA

There are about 260 crab apple trees with over 100 different cultivars around the Central Experimental Farm. Many were planted in the early years of the Arboretum and still remain, but a large proportion are 'Rosyblooms'. This is the name given by the former Dominion Horticulturist, W. T. Macoun, to the series bred here in the 1920s by Isabella Preston, who named her trees after Canadian lakes. Alongside Prince of Wales Drive in the Arboretum there are 'Cowichan', 'Rousseau' and others. On the other side of the road, bordering the Ornamental Gardens, there are many 'Makamik' and 'Arrow'. Elsewhere there is a 'Simcoe' and a 'Sissipuk', trees she bred and planted in 1928.

Isabella Preston also became internationally renowned for her irises, lilacs and lilies.

Top: 'Makamik' blossoms
Right, top: 'Zumi' (foreground),
Rosyblooms (rear)
Right, bottom: 'Red Jade'

Malus baccata

SIBERIAN CRAB APPLE

"Although many new crab apples have originated from this species as one of the parents, none of its progeny can produce such year-round beauty. In spring it is covered with white flowers, in summer its green leaves produce abundant shade, in fall the leaves take on a vibrant autumn hue and its small fruits hang on long after the new year has been heralded." A.R. BUCKLEY, FORMER CURATOR OF THE ARBORETUM

Leaves are simple and alternately-arranged. Flowers are bisexual.

The Siberian Crab Apple has spread around the world from the valleys of big rivers flowing north and east through central and eastern Asia. It dominates woodlands where there are dense, lower layers of shrubby cherries, hawthorns, and willows. It tolerates a variety of soils, but needs good drainage. It is extremely cold-hardy and is drought resistant. Siberian Crab Apple wood is hard, fine-textured and strong but its use is limited because of the small logs.

Although the Siberian Crab Apple faces many pests and diseases, old trees are common in cities and towns. The Arboretum has a fine old specimen in the Circle. Younger ones are found alongside the Rideau Canal.

ANCESTOR TO MANY CRAB APPLE VARIETIES

Using the Siberian Crab Apple, hundreds of cultivars were developed for flowers and fruit in Canada, Europe, and Russia. In 1887, the Director of the Central Experimental Farm, Dr William Saunders, began the earliest Canadian project to breed apples that were hardy enough for the prairies. He imported Siberian Crab Apple seeds from Russia and in

continued…

The Siberian Crab Apple grows for many decades, but it never becomes a tall tree. The crown consists of many thin branches and twigs.

A widely spread crown and short, multiple trunks or large limbs are distinctive features of this tree.

Small, cherry-size fruit remain on trees well after leaves have fallen. Unlike other apple trees, the crab apple drops sepals from fruit tops.

Malus baccata

SIBERIAN CRAB APPLE

Continued from page 174

1894, when the surviving seedlings had begun
flowering, the first breeding was done using
pollen from large-fruiting eastern apple trees.

Birds and small animals consume the
crab apples. Mr. Buckley wrote in 1967, "It so
happens that its fruits, which persist nearly all
winter, are rated by the bird population as the
best of any tree in the Arboretum." Rodents and
rabbits chew the bark of young trees in winter.

Bark is thin and smooth on
young trees. On old trees,
it is thin and split into
irregular, flat plates.

Corylus colurna
TURKISH HAZEL

The old Turkish Hazel in the photo is in the maple section. In the Arboretum in 1899, the species was rated as "tender," meaning that in winter its wood was killed to the snow line or to the ground. Hardier stock came later. In 1980, A.R. Buckley, former Curator of the Arboretum, described "lovely little trees 7.5 to 9m high, with perfect conical outlines" and recommended the Turkish Hazel as "a perfectly formed tree for small homes."

BEAUTIFUL SPRING CATKINS

Craggy and tall, the current Turkish Hazel in the Arboretum is a far cry from a "lovely little tree." It does, however, still have the ornamental feature of "slender pendulous catkins which are borne in the fall but burst forth in early spring, when the anthers break into soft yellow cascades of beauty." (Buckley, 1980)

Turkish Hazels grow naturally in the moist forests of south-eastern Europe and western Asia. Along with apple and yew trees, they form an understorey in the forest below tall oak, beech and chestnut trees. Turkish Hazel tolerates partial shade and occasionally dry soil, but it needs moist and fertile soil to produce nuts. Its wood is hard, heavy, and strong, with a reddish colour which makes it highly attractive to furniture makers.

Alternate, simple leaves remain green all summer, even during a very dry season, and turn pale brown in the fall.

It has long, lower branches close to the ground forming a wide base for a pyramid, mostly of upper branches.

k. gier

TASTY IN DESSERTS

The Turkish Hazel has been widely planted recently in North America as both an ornamental and a nut producer. All species of hazel, also known as filberts, produce edible nuts. Turkey is the largest producer of commercial hazelnuts, especially popular for use in desserts. Because of its non-suckering habit, the Turkish Hazel often provides the stock on which commercial hazelnuts (Common Hazel, *Corylus avellana*) are grown as grafts.

A Turkish Hazel tree has a tall, straight trunk and dense, symmetrical crown.

The bark is thin and scaly on big trees.

Male flower catkins are noticeable in early spring on the ends of peripheral twigs. Tiny female flowers grow on the same tree, becoming more conspicuous when they start to produce the rounded nuts.

Turkish Hazel trees are almost pest and disease free. Their nuts have hard shells, which still do not stop squirrels from consuming most of the annual crop. Pruning or trimming is rarely needed. Because of its resistance to pollution and drought, this tree could be used in most urban settings. A Turkish Hazel tree can be difficult to start, but once started it will be easy to grow for decades.

Carya ovata
SHAGBARK HICKORY

Shiny, hairless, compound leaves have 5 to 7 leaflets.

Also known as Upland or Bird's-eye Hickory, mature Shagbark Hickory trees have become very handsome in the Arboretum. This is mainly due to their delicate, dangling catkins in spring, deep shade in summer, and yellow-gold colours in the fall. The oldest tree (shown in the photo) grows beside Birch Avenue near the Saunders building. A fine specimen can be found just north of Building 74 and some cultivars were planted more recently in the Circle.

Besides its ornamental attributes, this tree is of great value, as are all hickories, for the high quality of its wood. It is included in the Fruit category here because of the importance of its edible nuts. In a good year, a Shagbark Hickory can produce 70 pounds of nuts, providing food for a variety of wildlife. The nuts have been a staple of many First Nations peoples, who ground and boiled the kernels to use in cornbread and cornmeal mush.

GROWS SLOWLY ALONGSIDE MANY DECIDUOUS TREES

The natural range of Shagbark Hickory in eastern North America overlaps those of Black Walnut and Butternut. It grows alongside oaks, ash, maples and other deciduous trees. A slow-growing species, Shagbark Hickory prefers deep, fertile and moist soils. It needs little light; its young trees tolerate shade for many years.

Fungal diseases and insect damage are common but not fatal. Weather extremes, either cold or drought, are the major destructive threats to this tree.

A straight trunk is covered by many long, grey, plate-like strips of bark. The tree was named for this shaggy bark.

The Shagbark Hickory is a medium-sized tree, rarely exceeding 20 m in height.

A thick, four-ribbed husk embraces a nearly round nut. Mature, light grey nuts, 2 to 3 cm in length, fall off the tree when husks open in early autumn.

Male catkins (left) and spikes of small female flowers appear before the leaves are fully developed.

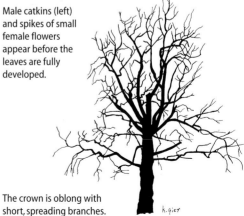

The crown is oblong with short, spreading branches.

Sorbus aucuparia

EUROPEAN MOUNTAIN ASH

Large clusters of brightly coloured berries are a major attraction of the European Mountain Ash. Initially bitter, the berries become sweet after the first frosts, and birds and small animals quickly remove the fruit. *Aucuparia*, from the Latin word meaning 'to catch birds', refers to the appeal of this tree to birds.

European Mountain Ash trees were first planted in the Arboretum in 1889. A very old specimen is near the William Saunders Building by Birch Avenue. Young cultivars are growing at the north and south ends of the Arboretum.

MORE THAN BEAUTIFUL BERRIES

Also known as the Rowan Tree, the European Mountain Ash has other attractions. The flowers are showy, the tree grows rapidly but remains small, and it has a graceful shape and beautiful leaves. It is a popular ornamental, extensively used in environmentally friendly architecture and landscaping.

Another common name is Witchwood. According to the folklore of some European countries, this tree can ward off evil spirits if planted around homes, or if sprigs of branches are hung above entrance doors.

Originating in Europe and northern Asia, European Mountain Ash trees form a lower layer in mixed forests dominated by birch, spruce, pine, and aspen. It is also found in forest glades surrounded by oak, linden, maple, and other broad-leafed trees. Full sun is needed for flowering and fruiting, and European Mountain Ash grows better on moist, fertile lowlands than on dry, sandy uplands.

Fire blight, canker, and borers can affect growth of both young and mature trees, but good soil, full sun and few pollutants will keep trees healthy for years.

Alternate leaves are compound with an uneven number of leaflets.

Bark is thin and smooth for almost the entire life span of this tree.

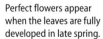

Perfect flowers appear when the leaves are fully developed in late spring.

A European Mountain Ash quickly reaches its maximum height. A well-established tree often has several trunks, with young ones replacing the old.

Berries remain on trees from late summer to early winter, depending on the birds.

Upright, thick branches and stout twigs form a rounded crown, which becomes irregular on older trees.

Morus alba

WHITE MULBERRY

Leaves are up to 15 cm long and simple, varying in shape from non-lobed to irregularly multiple-lobed. The top surface of the leaf is smooth and shiny.

A feature of the Circle area of the Arboretum is a Weeping White Mulberry (*Morus alba* 'Pendula'), planted in 1895. In winter, its gnarled, uneven trunk and twisting branches are striking, and in spring its fresh young leaves provide a delightful contrast to those rough shapes. Near this specimen are young, weeping cultivars. A mature White Mulberry tree, shown in the drawing, and in the bark photo, can be found in the Campus area beside Maple Drive.

The White Mulberry has had such a long history of cultivation in China that it is unclear what its natural environment really is. It needs full sun, tolerates drought and extreme cold, resists urban pollution and will grow in various types of soil. It is, therefore, highly valued as an ornamental, especially the weeping cultivars.

HOME OF THE CHINESE SILKWORM

White Mulberry trees have been the home of the Chinese silkworm for over five thousand years.

Although the prime use of White Mulberry was silk production, there have been, and continue to be, many other uses for the tree. Valued in China for its timber, when established in North America the species became important for its fruit.

A TREE FOR THE BIRDS

"When in fruit it is a tremendous attraction to all kinds of birds. In the Arboretum … the fruits are quickly devoured by robins," observed A.R. Buckley, former Curator of the Arboretum, in 1967. White Mulberry trees are sometimes considered a nuisance because fruit left by the birds can make a mess. Fruitless cultivars are available to solve this problem. Powdery mildew, leaf spots, and bacterial blight are often present but these trees are rarely affected by anything more damaging.

The bark is orange-brown when young, becoming grey with age.

This old Weeping White Mulberry, less than 2 m high, is an ornamental cultivar. It has all the characteristics (leaves, flowers, fruit) of the species, except for its shape and size.

Male flowers are catkins. Spiky female flowers produce juicy, berry-like fruit in late summer. Fruit do not all ripen at once.

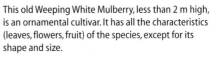

k. gier

The White Mulberry never grows high, but its trunk may reach over 50 cm in diameter. Its crown is rounded, consisting of many thin branches.

(Above and next page)
Bebb's Oak (*Quercus × bebbiana*)

Oaks form one of the largest collections in the Arboretum, with 29 varieties, many represented by a number of specimens. This was also the case in the early days of the Arboretum; in 1904, there were 98 oak species and varieties.

A picturesque collection of oaks is found at the south end of the Arboretum including Scarlet, Shin, Bur, Basket, English, and Red Oaks. And then there is Bebb's Oak! This much-loved tree, with its great girth, huge spread and breathtaking canopy, dominates the area. According to Arthur Buckley (1980), the tree was collected from woodlands nearby and replanted here in 1898. It is a natural hybrid (*Quercus × bebbiana*) of White Oak (*Q. alba*), which is rare in the Ottawa valley, and Bur Oak (*Q. macrocarpa*), which is common to the region.

All oaks grow to become big, strong trees. They provide solid, durable and beautiful wood, used in construction, fine furniture and for many other purposes.

ACORNS IN ONE OR TWO YEARS

White oaks and red oaks can be found throughout the Arboretum. The most visible difference between these two types is the length of time they take to make an acorn. White oaks produce an acorn that is ready in one year while red oaks take two years. In early spring, half-formed acorns can already be seen on red oak twigs, while there will be no sign yet of acorns on the white oaks.

White oaks in the Arboretum included in this book are Bur Oak (*Quercus macrocarpa*), English Oak (*Q. robur*), Basket or Chestnut Oak (*Q. prinus*) and Swamp White Oak (*Q. bicolor*). Red oaks are Pin Oak (*Q. palustris*), Red Oak (*Q. rubra*) and Scarlet Oak (*Q. coccinea*).

Quercus bicolor
SWAMP WHITE OAK

Simple, alternate leaves have short stalks and many shallow rounded lobes. Leaves are much lighter in colour underneath than on top.

Acorns grow on long stalks either singly, like the immature one in the photo, or in pairs. A cap covers less than one third of a mature acorn, which ripens in one season and germinates in the fall.

Swamp White Oaks are rare in Canada. The Latin name *bicolor*, meaning two colours, refers to the leaf with its dark, shiny green on the upper surface and lighter green on the underside. The species was first planted in the Arboretum in 1897. Two tall, broad Swamp White Oaks, dating from 1939, are side by side at the northern end of the Arboretum near the magnolia collection.

The natural habitats of the Swamp White Oak are the floodplains, swamp borders and poorly-drained moist sites in the middle of the North American continent. It grows with maples, ash, hickories and other deciduous trees. A Swamp White Oak needs full or partial sun to dominate in forests and to produce its sweet and nutritious acorns.

LARGE CROP OF ACORNS EVERY FEW YEARS

A favourite food for deer, bears, many rodents and birds, the acorns are produced in abundant crops every 3 to 5 years. Many insects and fungi are associated with this species, but no one damaging agent is critical.

Swamp White Oak trees are often seen in parks, but tend to be too broad for use as street trees. Their wood is hard and heavy, and like that of other oaks, it has multiple applications in construction, cabinet making, packing and shipbuilding.

fyi *Swamp White Oak is a large tree that may live over 200 years without showing any decline.*

Large lower branches will often remain on the tree and make the crown irregular and wide-spreading.

k gier

Swamp White Oak bark is coarse and scaly on the trunk and limbs of mature trees.

Greenish male catkins and reddish female flowers emerge at the same time as leaves.

Quercus coccinea
SCARLET OAK

Simple leaves are deeply lobed, and each lobe has a bristle at the tip.

Two mature Scarlet Oaks grow at close quarters with English and Red Oaks in the oak area at the southern part of the Arboretum near Prince of Wales Drive, and a young one can also be seen nearby. The Scarlet Oak 'Splendens' shown in the photo, dating from 1962, is found to the north, on the slope between the old Windbreak and Building 72.

POPULAR FOR LANDSCAPING

Leaves of the Scarlet Oak are red when they first appear in the spring, turn to a bright green in summer and in the fall they become reddish again, somewhere between maroon and a brilliant scarlet. With such colourful leaves and their round, textured crowns, Scarlet Oaks are popular in city landscaping in North America and Europe. They grow up to 25m in height.

Scarlet Oaks are native to eastern North America, growing with other oak species on dry upland sites. They tolerate poor and dry soils, but need lots of light to grow and regenerate. Periodic fires or intensive grazing will cause Scarlet Oaks to dominate in forests. As with other oaks in the red oak group, the wood of the Scarlet Oak is less valuable than white oak lumber.

Scarlet Oak acorns are a very important food source for many animals and birds, including game species. Deer consume the young shoots of this oak when other food is scarce. Scarlet Oak is a host tree for dangerous defoliators such as the Forest Tent Caterpillar and the Gypsy Moth. These insects and winter dieback can suppress the growth or destroy the trees. Vigorous stump sprouts, however, can replace damaged trees.

Male catkins and spikes of female flowers appear at the same time as leaves.

New acorn

Scarlet Oak is a fast-growing, relatively short-living tree.

Acorns are small and become mature at the end of the second growing season after pollination.

k.gier

The bark is thin on old trees with shallow furrows and ridges.

Its crown consists of many thin, upright branches that cast a good shade.

Quercus macrocarpa
BUR OAK

The tip and upper lobes form the widest part of the leaf.

Bur Oak trees are often as wide as they are tall.

h. gier

"This large, stately, native oak with its tall trunk and spreading branches," as described in 1980 by A.R. Buckley, former Curator of the Arboretum, can be admired for its grandeur and enjoyed for its shade at several locations around the Arboretum.

The Bur Oak in the photo is found by the path below the Eastern Lookout. A giant, old Bur Oak grows in the Woodlands next to the Hosta Garden and there is another beautiful one at the bottom of the slope down from the Southern Lookout. A solitary Bur Oak, like the one in the Central Experimental Farm field west of Fisher Avenue, is a common sight in the fields of rural eastern Ontario.

ALSO KNOWN AS MOSSY CUP OAK
Bur (or Burr) Oak is also called Mossy Cup Oak, because of the fringed cup that almost encloses the acorn. That was the name the tree was given in the 1899 catalogue of trees in the Arboretum. Another common name is Blue Oak.

The Bur Oak has a huge range from Canada to the Gulf of Mexico. Within Canada, this native white oak is found from New Brunswick to southern Saskatchewan. It can be a tall tree where the soil is fertile and fresh, or a low shrub on dry rocky bluffs. Its wood has a high commercial value, for example for flooring and furniture.

This oak is exceptionally resistant to city air pollution. The wide spread of its branches makes the tree unsuitable for street plantings but provides welcoming shade in public parks.

The large acorns of the Bur Oak are an important food source for birds and animals. They are also edible for humans and somewhat sweet. First Nations people consumed the kernels raw or prepared them by boiling or roasting the acorns.

Mature acorns are big, up to 4 cm long. A fringed cap or "mossy cup" covers more than half their length.

Bark is thick and
deeply furrowed.

Male (pollen) flowers,
shown here, are yellow-
green catkins. Female
(seed) flowers are reddish
and grow in small spikes
of 1 to 3 flowers.

Quercus palustris
PIN OAK

Alternately-arranged leaves turn red in fall, then become brown and stay on the tree almost all winter.

Small branches and slender twigs create a fine-textured crown. The small branches are strong and stiff.

k.gier

A couple of fine young Pin Oaks that produce acorns are close to the Southern Path near the hawthorn collection. W.T. Macoun, former Dominion Horticulturist, in 1925 reported that at least one Pin Oak had been a success in the Arboretum, but generally it had not done as well in Ottawa as the Red Oak. "The Pin Oak, because of its smaller and more cut foliage, is a more graceful tree than the Red, and the leaves colour very highly in autumn."

The Pin Oak is native to eastern and central North America, growing in bottomlands in pure stands or together with White Oak, American Elm, Red Maple, and other hardwood trees. Pin Oaks tolerate floods occurring before or after the growing season, and grow well on poorly aerated clay soils. This tree produces high-quality hardwood, known on the market under the general name of "red oak."

BEAUTIFUL, DEEPLY GROOVED LEAVES

Pin Oak grows quickly, as compared with other oak species, and is a relatively short living tree. The species has many ornamental applications due to the texture of its crown and the colours of its fall leaves. "The beautiful, deeply grooved leaves of this species throw a checkered shade, a factor that makes this oak desirable as a tree for the street or for shade on a lawn." (Buckley, 1980)

Pin Oak acorns, because of their small size and thin shells, are great food for migrating ducks. Many rodents also eat the acorns and thin bark of young trees. As with many oaks, diseases and pests damage trees, but rarely kill them. Pruning of lower branches may be needed on lawns.

For most of the Pin Oak's life, its crown is pyramidal with long descending lower branches and erect upper ones.

Male catkins (above) and clusters of female flowers grow separately on the same tree. Leaves appear on new growth; mature acorns are always on the prior year's twigs.

The bark is thin, even on mature trees.

Pin Oak acorns are small. They become ripe at the end of their second growing season.

Quercus prinus
CHESTNUT OAK

Alternate leaves are shiny above and hairy below.

A "handsome and striking oak," according to A.R. Buckley, former Curator of the Arboretum, the Chestnut Oak species was first planted in the Arboretum in 1889. Specimens can now be found in the oak section and also on the slope down to the old Windbreak.

Also known as Basket Oak, it is native to North America. It grows slowly and rarely becomes a large tree regardless of age and site conditions. It originates in the Appalachian Mountains where it forms sparse forests on dry, infertile soils on the tops of ridges and uplands. It also grows with Table Mountain Pine, hemlock, and other oak species.

SWEET ACORNS

In landscaping, it is a useful tree for shade and decoration on bare land and dry sites, such as parking lots. Its heavy, strong and durable wood is excellent for exterior and interior construction and finishing.

The sweet acorns of Chestnut Oak trees are a favourite food for many animals, large and small, including the black bear. Gypsy Moth and other pests and diseases common to oaks infest this species, but rarely kill trees. Many sprouts emerge from stumps to rejuvenate old trees.

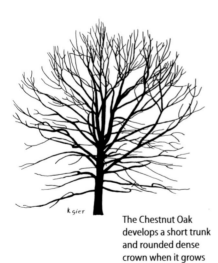

The Chestnut Oak develops a short trunk and rounded dense crown when it grows on an open site.

Male catkins (in photo) and spikes of female flowers grow on the same tree.

Bark is initially thin, becoming thick and coarse with flat-topped ridges.

These young Chestnut Oak acorns will grow to be among the largest of all those of native oaks. They become chestnut-brown when ripe at the end of the growing season.

Quercus robur

ENGLISH OAK

Leaves are simple with rounded lobes and distinctive ears close to a very short stalk. Copper-coloured leaves remain on the tree until the early spring.

Acorns, from 1.5 to 2.5 cm long, are borne from tiny, stalkless female flowers. The acorns develop long stalks (peduncles), often two times longer than the seed itself. Because of this, the tree has been given the common name Pedunculate Oak.

Oak forests once covered much of England. The English Oak became the stuff of legend in that country — from the wood of the table of King Arthur to the woods of Robin Hood and his merry men. The English Oak is native to mixed woodlands across Europe and western Asia. In central Russia there are English Oak plantations that are 400 years old. One early specimen in the Arboretum grew from an acorn collected by a traveller in Russia.

The oldest English Oaks now in the Arboretum are in the oak area beside Prince of Wales Drive. Others can be found near the old Windbreak and in the Campus area. In the mid 1950s cultivars of English Oak, such as the tall and slim *Quercus robur* f. *fastigiata*, were planted at the northern tip of the Arboretum beside Prince of Wales Drive. Several young narrow-crown cultivars can also be seen at the southern end of the Arboretum.

Such cultivars are better suited for planting along narrow city streets. The species English Oak, which is broad, round and tall, is often used in parks. It is very tolerant of urban pollution and requires little maintenance in a sunny space. Because of its shape and its extensive anchor roots, planting in small shaded spots or in proximity to buildings is not advised.

KNOWN TO LIVE OVER A THOUSAND YEARS

Slow growing and very long lived, some English Oaks have been known to live over 1,000 years. Introduced to North America in colonial times, it prefers basic, well-drained and fertile soils, but can grow on poor acid and sandy soils as well. English Oak timber in Canada has had many important uses, such as for oak paneling, shipbuilding and the manufacture of railway carriages. Acorns are high protein food for animals and birds.

Mature trees are tall and their strong branches form rounded, broad crowns. Extensive anchor roots allow trees to survive summer droughts and resist strong winds.

The bark is thick, grey-black and furrowed with vertical ridges.

The English Oak often has irregular branches.

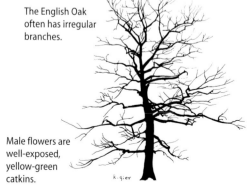

Male flowers are well-exposed, yellow-green catkins.

Quercus rubra

RED OAK

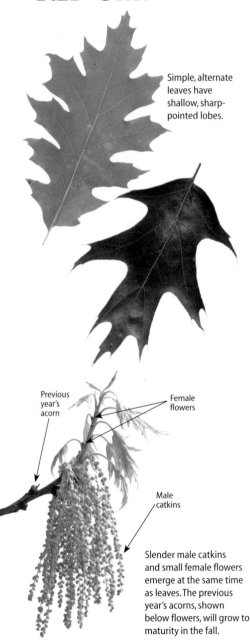

Simple, alternate leaves have shallow, sharp-pointed lobes.

Previous year's acorn

Female flowers

Male catkins

Slender male catkins and small female flowers emerge at the same time as leaves. The previous year's acorns, shown below flowers, will grow to maturity in the fall.

A beautiful, spreading Red Oak can be seen on the main lawn of the Campus area, in front of the William Saunders Building. This tree was planted in 1911 by the Governor General of Canada, Prince Arthur, the Duke of Connaught. Red Oaks of similar vintage are in the Woodlands and at the southern end of the Arboretum. It was one of the first species to be planted in the Arboretum.

LARGE, GLOSSY LEAVES THAT TURN RED IN THE FALL

The official tree of Prince Edward Island, the Red Oak is hardy and fast-growing. A native North American tree, it is found in mixed and deciduous forests from Eastern Canada to the mid-east U.S. It will grow in light, sandy soils, but not in heavy, wet soils. Red Oaks also grow in plantations, on farm lands, and provide shade in parks and urban green spaces.

The leaves of the Red Oak are large and very glossy. The tree gets its name from their colour in the fall.

GREAT FOR A SWING OR A TREE HOUSE

In the forest, a Red Oak is likely to be narrow and tall, whereas in the open, such as on the Campus lawn, it has a thick trunk and wide crown. "If one has the space, these are the trees whose sturdy spreading branches are perfect for hanging a swing or building a tree house." (Blouin, 2001)

Red Oak wood is hard and strong, good for construction, furniture, pulp, firewood and many other applications. Acorns are bitter but abundant. Crops almost every year sustain populations of deer, rodents and birds. Many insects and fungi are associated with this species, but no one agent is a challenge to the tree's survival.

Red Oak trees grow fast and, if partially shaded, become very tall within 50 years.

Grey bark is smooth for many years. On older trees, the relatively thin bark becomes coarse with flat-topped ridges.

Acorns are up to 2 cm long with a very shallow cap. They drop from the tree in late summer and germinate later in the fall.

Big upright branches support a wide spreading crown.

Carya illinoinensis
PECAN

Alternate leaves consist of 9 to 19 sharply pointed leaflets with an asymmetrical base.

A green, four-ribbed husk encases an elongated 3 to 5 cm nut which, at maturity, is reddish-brown. The nut falls off the tree in early autumn when the husk turns brown and opens.

I t should not be growing in Ottawa, but there is a Pecan which has been growing in the Arboretum for over 20 years. The species was not tested there for hardiness in the early years. A.R. Buckley, former Curator of the Arboretum, refers to a Pecan tree planted in 1950 which did not show any sign of fruiting. The one Pecan that grows now in the Arboretum, near the southern end of the old Windbreak, was planted in 1984. It flowers almost every year, but the fruit fall before maturing.

Pecans are the largest of all *Carya* species, growing up to 30 m high in the southern United States. The specimen in the Arboretum is about 10 m high. The species grows naturally in the Mississippi Valley of the U.S., and has been widely planted throughout the U.S. Most of the world's pecan nut supply is produced on plantations in the southern states, especially Texas and Georgia.

Open hardwood forests and riverfront ridges are prime natural sites for the Pecan. It tolerates summer droughts, if soils are deep and fertile. Full sun is needed for a healthy tree and abundant nut crops.

THE SWEETEST NUTS

The Pecan has the sweetest of all nuts, an extreme opposite to the Bitternut Hickory. Pecans are a prized ingredient in many food products. Pecan groves sustain wildlife populations with food and safe nesting sites. Squirrels are not popular in Pecan orchards because they will consume a large portion of the crop. Pecan wood has little commercial value.

Extremely cold weather and sustained drought are the two prime problems of Pecan plantations. Fungal disease and insect damage are not major concerns.

The Pecan is a large, slow-growing tree. This Pecan in the Arboretum, over 20 years of age, is growing even more slowly than those in natural habitats.

Bark is grey and rough. Unlike that of other *Carya* species, bark on the Pecan does not become loose with corky plates.

Spikes of tiny female flowers appear later, on tips of current year shoots.

In early summer, yellow-green male catkins show up on the previous year's twigs.

In their natural habitats, trees can have trunks almost 2 m in diameter and vast, irregular crowns.

k. gier

Pinus cembra
SWISS STONE PINE

Needles are relatively short, straight, green or blue-green, and occur in bundles of five.

A distinguishing feature of the Swiss Stone Pine is its thick, compact habit, which makes it highly desirable for ornamental purposes. The tree in the photograph is found between the Canada Agriculture Museum and the greenhouses at Building 75, beside the Ornamental Gardens. Other beautiful Swiss Stone Pines can be seen in the Circle area of the Arboretum near the Weeping White Mulberry and Balsam Fir trees. A unique hedgerow of Swiss Stone Pine has been growing in the old hedge collection since 1894. Some of the trimmed trees there have produced cones, but without viable seeds.

PICTURESQUE AND SLOW GROWING

The picturesque Swiss Stone Pine is a personal favourite of Trevor Cole, former Curator of the Arboretum, who likes "the way it keeps its lower branches right down to the ground and doesn't develop the bare stem that so many of the pines do." (Cole, 1991) It is slow-growing. Twenty-five years after being planted in the Arboretum, a Swiss Stone Pine was reported to be just 2 m wide at the base of the crown and 6 m high.

VALUED FOR ITS PINE NUTS

The Swiss Stone Pine came to North America from the European Alps and Carpathian Mountains. In those areas, people collect the seeds (or pine nuts) for food. Animals and birds also consume the seeds. No major pests or diseases have been reported but, like others in the 5-needle or white pine group, this species is susceptible to White Pine Blister Rust.

The Swiss Stone Pine will survive a harsh climate if exposed to full sunlight. Soil must be well drained, but not necessarily fertile. This tree

The scaly, grey-brown bark becomes exposed on older trees.

The Swiss Stone Pine has many large branches. Crowns of the young trees are narrow, conical, and, unlike the crowns on other pines, these are very dense.

does not grow well in heavy clay soil. Wood of the Swiss Stone Pine has had limited commercial use because, in their natural habitats, they tend to grow sparsely, in remote areas. In North America, major botanical gardens and city parks grow this attractive tree, although cultivation in cities can be limited by pollution.

Mature cones are almost round. Purple-brown, resinous scales tightly cover large, wingless seeds. Cones remain on the tree unless birds or animals destroy them.

Pinus koraiensis
KOREAN PINE

Stiff needles grow in bundles of five and remain on the trees for 3 to 4 years.

Immature and mature cones are resinous, but scales open easily.

In 1924, W.T. Macoun, former Dominion Horticulturist, wrote that the Korean Pine "is very attractive in appearance and should be more extensively planted as an ornamental." This has indeed happened and the tree is enjoyed around the world in city parks of all sizes where it is not exposed to pollution.

A COMPACT, ELEGANT, FIVE-NEEDLE PINE

Like those of the white pines, the needles of the Korean Pine grow in clusters of five. The Korean Pine tree is more compact and slower growing than other white pines. While it is a large tree in its natural habitat, it is relatively small in parks. The two beautiful Korean Pines in the Circle area of the Arboretum near the Eastern Lookout, are about half the size of two nearby Western White Pines, although they were all planted around 1950. At about the same time, the Canadian Forest Services established a Korean Pine plantation at the Ottawa Research Station near Mer Bleu, and the remaining trees there are larger than the two in the Arboretum.

ABUNDANT CROPS OF PINE NUTS

Korean Pines came to North American parks and plantations from the temperate mixed forests of northeast Asia. In that region they join with spruce, fir, elm and linden in stands that exist without apparent change for centuries. A Korean Pine will tolerate poor, sandy and gravel soils, and grows slowly even on nutrient-rich, moist soils. Korean Pine wood is light and strong. It is used for exterior construction, furniture, and interior finishing, but is rare on North American markets.

Korean Pine is also known as Korean Nut Pine because of the big, nutritious seeds that occur in abundant crops every 3 to 5 years. Birds and animals, including bears, forage

for these nuts. The dense crowns of the trees shelter birds and small rodents all year round. In cultivation, Korean Pines do not have serious diseases and pests. As with other five-needle pines, however, White Pine Blister Rust and root rot fungi are threats.

Korean Pines are large trees in the forest, much smaller in parks. Their crowns are symmetrical and narrow with slightly upturned branches.

The bark consists of irregular flakes and is relatively thin.

The wind carries pollen from pink male cones in early summer to fertilize purplish female cones. Seeds, which are wingless, become ripe in the fall of the second growing season.

Juglans nigra
BLACK WALNUT

Leaves are compound, 30 to 60 cm long, with 14 to 22 long-pointed leaflets. The topmost leaflet is often missing or much smaller than the others.

The Black Walnut is valued for nuts and timber and also as an ornamental tree. The edible nuts retain their flavour when used in baked goods. Many birds enjoy them as well, usually relying on squirrels to open the hard shells.

A VALUABLE NATIVE WOOD

Black Walnut trees were among the first to be planted in the forest belt experiments at the Farm beginning in 1888. A group of Black Walnut trees continues to grow and regenerate alongside Fisher Avenue. James Fletcher, former Dominion Botanist and Entomologist, described it as "one of the most valuable of our native woods." The wood is highly prized in cabinet-making for its colour and grain.

As ornamentals, Black Walnut trees were first planted in the Arboretum in 1889. They have a handsome, graceful shape and their large, compound leaves cast a dappled shade allowing grass to grow underneath. Because of its durability and beauty, the Black Walnut is often used by landscapers in large urban settings. The oldest specimens in the Arboretum can be found in the Circle area. Some new cultivars are located in the nut collection at the east side of the Arboretum.

The Black Walnut is a native of mixed broad-leaved forests growing on fertile, well-drained soils in eastern North American regions. The life span of a Black Walnut tree may exceed 400 years. Its root system penetrates well below the surface of the soil. This helps to maintain stability in high winds despite its large crown. No fungi or insect pests damage this tree. The Black Walnut releases a chemical toxin (juglone) as a natural defence against competition, which prevents some plants from growing beneath the tree.

Fruit are round with yellow-green husks. Female flower parts are visible on top of these young ones.

Black Walnut trees grow to over 30 m in height and up to 2 m in trunk diameter when planted on favourable sites.

The dark brown bark, 5 to 7.5 cm thick, is deep-furrowed with broad ridges.

The dark brown nut shell within the husk is rough and very hard.

Hanging clusters of male flowers (catkins) are notable; female flowers are not noticeable.

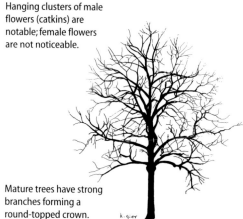

Mature trees have strong branches forming a round-topped crown.

Juglans ailantifolia
JAPANESE WALNUT

Compound leaves are 60 to 90 cm long with an uneven number of leaflets. Hairy, green husks (below) contain nuts encased in hard shells.

Also known as Heartnut, the Japanese Walnut tree was introduced to North America in the late 19th century, and now grows in nut plantations and as an ornamental. It originates in cool, temperate forests in Japan and other parts of far east Asia, and is one of many deciduous trees occurring in areas dominated by beech trees. Moist, sunny sites with deep soils are best for the Japanese Walnut to produce an abundant crop of nuts.

BOLD, BEAUTIFUL LEAF PATTERNS

A feature of the Japanese Walnut is the large, bold, composite leaf, beautifully decorative in the canopy of the tree. The Latin *ailantifolia* is derived from *ailanthus* or 'Tree of Heaven' and *folia*, meaning 'leaves'. A wide-spreading Japanese Walnut tree, dating from 1915, grows in the centre of the Circle among the Black Walnuts. The large size of the leaves is especially noticeable when they are strewn beneath this tree in the fall. A younger specimen can be seen among the Butternuts and Black Walnuts in the nut collection southeast of the magnolia collection.

The high quality wood of the Japanese Walnut is light and soft, does not crack or break easily, and is used in cabinetmaking.

Japanese Walnut trees produce many oily, sweet nuts that are good food for humans and animals. Squirrels will often eat immature nuts. This walnut is similar to the Butternut, but is resistant to Butternut Canker, a dangerous fungus disease. For this reason, the Japanese Walnut or its hybrids have replaced the Butternut in some plantations.

The Japanese Walnut is a fast-growing tree during its first two or three decades.

The thick bark on old trees has flat, irregular ridges and deep furrows.

Leaves and flowers emerge at the same time in late spring. Male catkins grow on 2-year-old or 3-year old twigs; female flowers with red pistils grow in spikes on top of new shoots.

Its crown is wide, often because of a short main trunk and several large, ascending branches.

k.gier

TREES FOR ENVIRONMENTAL STRESS

Above: Bitternut Hickory nuts

In this category are trees that can withstand and overcome stressful environmental conditions. Ever since the Experimental Farm system and the Arboretum were established, information has been gathered on how tree planting can help mitigate the adverse effects of natural events such as extreme weather, and of agricultural, industrial and urban development.

All the trees included in this group have demonstrated an ability to cope with the particular environmental pressures of Ottawa. They have all been introduced to Ottawa and the surrounding region, coming from many different countries and natural growing conditions.

PROVIDING SHELTER

The clearing of forested lands made vast fields for the growing of corn, wheat, and other crops. At the same time, the destructive force of high winds became unchecked. Immediately after the Experimental Farms were created, experiments were begun to discover which trees made the best shelterbelts to protect farm crops, livestock, gardens, and dwellings. From 1888 to 1900, 1.3 million young trees and 7 tons of tree seeds were sent to farmers and settlers across Canada.

European Larch, Norway Spruce, Scots Pine and Austrian Pine were found to be useful, along with native trees, in moderating the impact of strong winds. Windbreaks of one or a few rows of such trees provided protection, preserved soil moisture from excessive evaporation in summer, and helped to build an even and deep snow blanket over the fields in winter.

Various types of windbreak have been planted at the Central Experimental Farm over the years. The latest to emerge, a joint

venture of Agriculture and Agri-Food Canada and Friends of the Central Experimental Farm, is along the western boundary at Merivale Road. Most of the trees being planted to protect experimental crops in the fields, shelter adjacent communities and beautify the surroundings, are native varieties.

FOR THE SOIL, THE AIR AND THE SHORELINE

Industrial and urban construction diminishes the growing capacity of soils. Few trees can return to disturbed sites without expensive soil reclamation. In Ottawa and vicinities, Manitoba Maple, Black Locust and Honey Locust trees are used as pioneers to diminish erosion and restore the fertility of bare ground, while providing shade for homes and streets.

The dense crowns of Littleleaf Linden and Bitternut Hickory help to purify the air and reduce sound pollution. This promotes the clean air and quiet preferred by homeowners in their residential areas.

It is hard to imagine a more harmonious connection between water and land than that which exists where there are White Willows. The roots of this tree keep the shoreline stable and its branches, hanging over the water, provide shelter for ducks and other creatures.

ENVIRONMENTAL

Carya cordiformis

BITTERNUT HICKORY

Alternate compound leaves turn yellow in the fall.

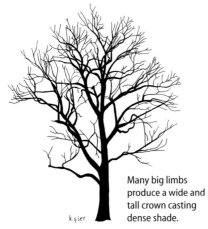

Many big limbs produce a wide and tall crown casting dense shade.

k.gier

Yes, the thin-shelled nuts of this hickory are indeed bitter! Squirrels will eat them — apparently as a last resort. Bitternut is considered, however, to be the finest hickory for smoking hams and bacon.

Also known as Swamp Hickory, the Bitternut Hickory is distinguished by its bright yellow winter buds. First planted as a species in the Arboretum in 1897, there is a giant Bitternut Hickory in the Woodlands area next to the Eastern Lookout. Down the slope towards Dow's Lake, there is a younger specimen. The vast, rigid crown is a safe place for the nests of both big and small birds. Diseases and pests rarely affect the appearance of these trees and their nut crops. The most common problem is heart rot, which carves big holes in old trunks.

HARDWOOD THAT IS STRONG, HEAVY AND SHOCK RESISTANT

Bitternut Hickories are North American native trees growing in most eastern deciduous forests except those in the high Appalachian Mountains. They often appear in small numbers in oak dominated old-growth forests. They tolerate poor and dry sites, but need deep fertile soils to produce nuts and massive trunks. Because of their large size and durability, Bitternut Hickories may be a good choice as a focal tree in landscaping projects.

The wood is hard, strong, heavy and shock-resistant. Besides its usefulness in smoking food and the warmth it generates in the fireplace, the wood is valued for making furniture, tool handles, golf clubs, baseball bats and drumsticks. It is relatively scarce, however, and difficult to work with, as compared with other hardwoods.

A thin husk and hard, whitish shell cover an oily, bitter kernel.

Bark is thin with rough, shallow ridges on older trees.

Bitternut Hickories, like this one near the Eastern Lookout, become large trees after decades of growth and stay firm and healthy for well over 100 years.

Unlike those on other hickories, Bitternut Hickory twigs have noticeable, bright yellow buds.

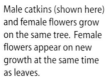

Male catkins (shown here) and female flowers grow on the same tree. Female flowers appear on new growth at the same time as leaves.

Gleditsia triacanthos
COMMON HONEY LOCUST

The delicate, attractive leaves of the Common Honey Locust are inviting, but the thorns of the tree are formidable. A.R. Buckley, former Curator of the Arboretum, wrote "Its fern-like, double-compound leaves … throw a light shade that allows grass to grow freely under the tree," but the "thorns on the trees are large and can be dangerous to children who attempt to climb into the branches."

Common Honey Locusts were widely planted to make windbreaks and shelterbelts, and such plantations helped to spread the tree beyond its natural habitat. The Common Honey Locust is a North American tree, although rarely found in Canada. It occurs naturally in woodlands dominated by oaks, west of the Appalachian Mountains. The species, along with Pecan, Black Walnut, and Kentucky Coffeetree, tends to be a minor component of old natural forests.

Mature Common Honey Locust trees are at the southern end of the Arboretum, across the path from the oaks. In the same area are some beautiful, golden-leaved varieties.

The first leaves are single compound. Double compound ones appear later on new growth. Both types of leaves consist of even numbers of alternately arranged leaflets. Big thorns arm the trunk, limbs, and vigorous twigs.

THORNLESS VARIETIES AVAILABLE

Because it is drought and salt tolerant, the Common Honey Locust is also planted alongside streets and parking lots. The development of thornless varieties has made it popular as an ornamental.

Common Honey Locust trees tolerate a variety of soils on both moist and dry sites, but need full sun and rich soil for best growth. The wood is hard, strong, and durable, making it popular for construction and wood-finishing projects.

Common Honey Locust flowers attract bees and other pollinators. Seeds in the pods are in a pulpy substance that tastes like honey (hence the tree's name). This is a favourite with wildlife, which spreads the seeds. It is a healthy tree, canker being the only threat.

Flowers are small and numerous, gathered in catkin-like inflorescences.

Bark is thin even on old Common Honey Locusts.

The Common Honey Locust rarely grows into a large tree, but is fast-growing at a young age. Wide, twisted pods (left) become noticeable in late summer and fall.

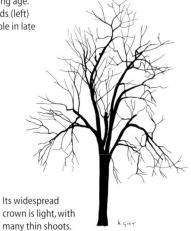

Its widespread crown is light, with many thin shoots.

Larix decidua
EUROPEAN LARCH

"The European Larch is a handsome tree, with upward curving horizontal branches from which hang smaller branches; the soft green foliage that covers these small branchlets is extremely graceful and beautiful in early spring." A.R. BUCKLEY, FORMER CURATOR OF THE ARBORETUM

First planted in the Arboretum in 1889, European Larch trees can now be found throughout the Central Experimental Farm. Several are near the Dominion Observatory building on Maple Drive at Carling Avenue. European Larches have succeeded on more diverse soils around the Farm than has the native Tamarack. Planted in the original forest belts along Carling and Fisher Avenues in 1888, European Larches proved to be among the fastest growing trees in that location.

As with other larch trees, there are two types of shoots, long and short, both of which lose their soft needles every fall.

A COMMON SIGHT IN PARKS

European Larch occurs naturally in high areas of the European Alps and Carpathian Mountains, where it grows beside Swiss Stone Pine, fir, or spruce. The European Larch avoids poor sandy soils, extremely wet sites and, at any age, it does not tolerate shade. Both healthy and handsome, the tree is a common specimen in European and North American parks.

European Larch wood is strong and durable. In foggy mountains, the larch log houses last the longest. Every few years, European Larch trees provide an abundant crop of seeds that are edible for birds and small animals.

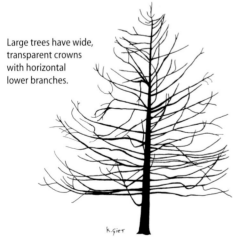

Large trees have wide, transparent crowns with horizontal lower branches.

k.gier

European Larch grows fast and has a relatively short lifespan.

A very thick bark, with corky flakes, develops as the tree ages.

Male and female cones grow next to each other on the same twigs. Female cones grow upright and are bigger than those of native larches.

Tilia cordata
LITTLELEAF LINDEN

"Say your vows under linden boughs." JOHN EASTMAN, 1992

Alternate heart-shaped leaves turn yellow in the fall.

Littleleaf Lindens are graceful, shapely trees with leaves that are smaller than those of other European lindens and Basswood (American Linden). The Littleleaf Linden is also more dense and can have an almost perfect pyramidal form, like the 15-year-old specimen in the Arboretum shown in the photo. As with other linden trees, the Littleleaf Linden is showy in mid-summer with many fragrant flowers in bloom, attracting a large number of bees.

A BEAUTIFUL SHADE TREE
In the northern section of the Arboretum, near the old Windbreak, there are some large, mature Littleleaf Lindens, as well as younger specimens, both of the species and cultivars. All told in the Arboretum, there are 12 varieties, in addition to the species itself. The Littleleaf Linden provides beautiful shade with its dense habit, illustrating why it has become so popular for planting in urban settings. This tree is used extensively in the landscaping of environment-friendly architecture, as well as in the design of parks.

fyi *In Greek and Roman mythology* Tilia cordata *symbolized wedded bliss and conjugal love.*

Trees grow quickly, forming dense crowns, which are pyramidal to rounded.

Littleleaf Lindens originate throughout European temperate forests, from northern Spain to the Ural Mountains. They occur on those sites where oaks, beech, elms, ash and maple trees grow to their fullest extent, and also in the northern spruce-fir forests of eastern Europe. The Littleleaf Linden tolerates a variety of soils and survives on flooded lowlands. Its light, soft, fine-grained wood is used for furniture, crafts and wood sculpture.

HONEY AND HONEYDEW
Littleleaf Linden flowers attract bees as well as other insects, and generate an excellent honey. The nut crop is usually abundant, providing food for small rodents and birds. This tree is

Hard, round, four-ribbed, small nuts remain on a tree well after the leaves have fallen.

easy to grow, with very few problems. Aphids deposit honeydew on leaves and stems, and Japanese beetles eat the leaves, but unless there is a severe infestation, trees survive these pests. Pruning of lower branches may be needed on lawns.

The lower branches of Littleleaf Linden trees are often the longest and grow close to the ground.

The bark has many long furrows and is strong and elastic. The inner bark was used in the past in eastern Europe for making shoes.

Yellowish flowers grow in clusters on a stalk attached to the lower part of a greenish bract.

Robinia pseudoacacia
BLACK LOCUST

"Except for its suckering habit and extremely brittle branches and branchlets, this would be an ideal tree for the impatient homeowner who seeks something that grows fast to nine metres and then stops."
A.R. BUCKLEY, FORMER CURATOR OF THE ARBORETUM

A splendid group of Black Locust trees grows at the south west side of the Arboretum with maples, horse chestnuts and oaks as neighbours. An early morning sky emphasizes the sharp irregular shape of the crowns of this group, making the structure of the trees particularly memorable. This tree species was first planted in the Arboretum in 1890. Lovely young Black Locust trees can be found beside the path east of the Woodlands and near the main parking lot.

KNOWN FOR DURABILITY
Native to the eastern United States and naturalized to southern Canada, the Black Locust has been readily used to reforest waste areas such as mine spoils where few trees would survive. Its hard, durable and rot-resistant timber was once used for fence posts and shipbuilding.

ORNAMENTAL USES TOO
Also serving as an ornamental tree, the Black Locust can be used as a focal point of a garden. Its clusters of fragrant flowers and delicate leaflets add beauty to any garden design. It is fast-growing, but rarely becomes tall and massive. With brittle twigs and branches, it can be damaged by ice and snow.

TENDENCY TO SPREAD
Placement of this tree is important because it can produce undesired new trees sprouting from the roots. Such suckers can wreak havoc on walkways, roads or walls in the vicinity.

Compound leaves have an uneven number of opposite leaflets which are smooth and oval.

fyi *The Latin name of this species honours Jean Robin, gardener to Henry IV of France.*

The bark of mature trees is thick and dark grey, with distinctive ridges.

Fragrant, showy flowers usually appear in June at the Arboretum.

k.gier

Seeds are abundant until new flowers bloom. Seed pods, of approximately 7 to 10 cm in length, remain during the winter.

This younger tree in the Arboretum has a more regular-shaped crown.

Acer negundo

Manitoba Maple

Manitoba Maple has pinnately compound leaves.
Because its leaves resemble those of the ash,
the tree is also known as Ashleaf Maple.
Pairs of winged seeds (below) remain on female trees
well after leaves have fallen.

The Manitoba Maple grows quickly and just about anywhere. It helps to control eroding soils and makes a fine shelterbelt. It was one of the first tree species planted in windbreaks and shelterbelts on Canadian prairie farms, with many of the seeds and seedlings distributed to farmers from the Experimental Farms.

A USEFUL TREE WITH BAD HABITS

In some areas, Manitoba Maples are considered to be invasive trees and are often called weed trees. This is because they shed large numbers of fertile seeds in late spring and seedlings appear in every nook and cranny. Furthermore, because the wood is weak and brittle, the Manitoba Maple is unattractive to loggers and unsuitable for children to climb on.

It is also known as Box-elder, where the "box" refers to its use as a hedge. It was planted as a hedge at the Farm in 1891, but William Saunders, first Director of the Farm, concluded that it was "too rank a grower here to make a neat hedge" without frequent clipping.

Mature trees can be seen now in the maple area and in other locations at the Arboretum, where the species was first planted in 1890. Despite its bad habits, "it makes a good lawn specimen … shows some fall colouring … will provide shade or a screen," wrote Arthur Buckley, former Curator of the Arboretum.

TOLERATES EXTREME COLD AND DROUGHT

Manitoba Maple is native to the Great Plains of North America. In woods, it grows together with Bur Oak, cottonwoods, ash trees, and willows. Although the tree tolerates extremely cold winters and is drought resistant, the best place for it to grow is in deep, moist soil on river banks and alongside lakes. Because city planners

Manitoba Maples grow and age quickly. The initial stem (or trunk) lives less than a century and is often replaced by new stems emerging from the stump or roots.

Clusters of male (in photo) and female flowers grow on different trees. They appear at the same time as leaves open up.

On young trees and on shoots, the bark is whitish, smooth and waxy. It becomes brown-grey and furrowed on big trunks and branches.

in the early days planted it along streets and property lines, and in parks, and because of its invasive habit, the Manitoba Maple expanded well beyond its natural range.

Flowers and seeds of the Manitoba Maple feed squirrels, chipmunks and birds. This species does face many diseases and pests, but they rarely kill the trees. Rotten trunks and big limbs break easily in wind or ice storms.

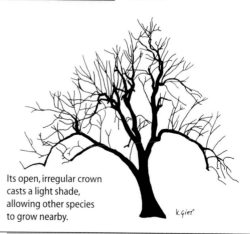

Its open, irregular crown casts a light shade, allowing other species to grow nearby.

Pinus nigra
AUSTRIAN PINE

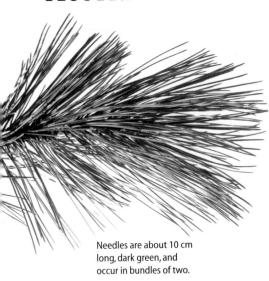

When their branches are able to spread, Austrian Pines can be excellent ornamental trees, with their dark green foliage and attractive form, though they can become irregularly shaped with age. The oldest Austrian Pines in the Arboretum grow in the Circle near the entrance. Dating from 1889, these were among the first trees to be planted here.

Needles are about 10 cm long, dark green, and occur in bundles of two.

OFTEN USED IN WINDBREAKS

With its dense branching system, the Austrian Pine has proven useful in shelterbelts and windbreaks. In the old Eastern Windbreak in the Arboretum, planted in the 1890s, Austrian Pines were combined with Ponderosa Pines, Scots Pines and Norway Spruce. A few specimens of Austrian Pine remain there. In another wind (and sound) break, young Austrian Pines are mixed with Red Pines and form thick clumps on hillocks at Dow's Lake next to the railway tunnel's ventilation house.

HARDY AND ADAPTABLE TO VARIOUS GROWING CONDITIONS

The Austrian Pine (also known as European Black Pine) was one of the earliest European conifers to be introduced into North America. It grows naturally in Mediterranean mountains on sites protected from weather extremes. It is indifferent to soil types, but growth is better on sandy soils with plenty of organic matter. Trees are well adapted to city environments and can withstand salt and drought. The Austrian Pine is one of the most commonly used ornamentals in cities and along highways.

The wood has commercial use in construction. Austrian Pine seeds are consumed by rodents and birds. Other parts of the tree are of little value to wildlife. This tree is not affected by major insect pests but fungal diseases can damage its roots, twigs and needles.

Austrian pine is a medium sized tree with a wide-spreading crown. Mature specimens grow to about 20 m.

Its thick bark consists of grey-brown ridges and dark brown furrows. These are almost black or *nigra*.

Immature female cones are shiny, yellow-brown, and symmetrical. They grow up to 5 to 7 cm long by the end of summer. Non-resinous scales easily disperse seeds in late fall and early winter.

Winter buds (left) are easy to distinguish by their woolly, white appearance at the ends of stout, upright twigs.

Pinus sylvestris
SCOTS PINE

Mature female cones release ripe seeds during the second winter after pollination.

Mature pines have high asymmetrical crowns like this one in front of the Heritage House, formerly the Dominion Animal Husbandman's residence.

Scots Pine trees adorn the Arboretum with their bright orange-brown bark, bluish-green needles and varied shapes. A distinctive crooked trunk, for example, can be seen on one old specimen in the Circle. Other beautiful Scots Pine are near the Eastern Lookout.

BOTH BEAUTIFUL AND FUNCTIONAL
In the forest belts first planted at the Farm in 1887, this species proved to be very successful for both timber and shelter. Around 25 Scots Pine trees remain in the old Windbreak planted in 1895 at the eastern edge of the Arboretum.

A LONG-LIVING TREE
Unlike many conifers, the way the Scots Pine grows can vary widely, from a tree with a tall single trunk to a twisted shrubby plant. Regardless of the form they take, Scots Pines grow for hundreds of years. Also known as Scotch Pines, they grow naturally in Europe and northern Asia tolerating various climatic and soil conditions from near-polar to almost Mediterranean. They were among the first trees to be introduced to North America.

Rapid growth, quality wood and shapely beauty have encouraged cultivation of this species in Canada for over a hundred years both in forest plantations and in recreational and urban settings. Unfortunately, Scots Pines can be seriously invasive pests that displace native vegetation.

Small animals and birds feed on its buds and seeds. Porcupines consume young bark and may seriously damage even big trees. Fungal diseases and insect damage to needles, buds and twigs are common, but only *Scleroderris* canker can be a serious problem.

Bright orange-brown bark covers more than half of the upper trunk (above). These trees are in the Windbreak near Dow's Lake. Lower bark (below) is thick and scaly.

Pairs of bluish-green twisted needles, 3 to 5 cm long, grow spirally on stout twigs.

Yellow male (left) and purplish female cones appear in early summer on the same tree.

fyi A fast-growing tree, it can reach 20 metres high in less than 80 years.

Picea abies
NORWAY SPRUCE

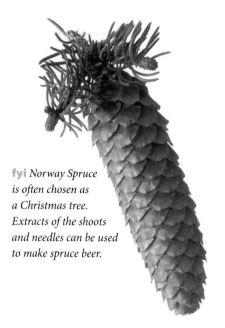

*fyi Norway Spruce
is often chosen as
a Christmas tree.
Extracts of the shoots
and needles can be used
to make spruce beer.*

Mature cones are larger (10 to 18 cm)
than those of any native spruce.

The majestic Norway Spruce tends to
dominate forests in its native areas of
northern, central and eastern Europe. In the
Arboretum, there are old specimens of weeping
and dwarf cultivers in the Circle area. The
group of Norway Spruce in the winter photo is
found on Maple Drive in front of the William
Saunders Building.

BEAUTY AND UTILITY
Fast growth and beauty make this species and its
cultivars a good choice for ornamental purposes
and it is frequently used in this way. It is also
used in reforestation. Its high-quality wood is
attractive for general carpentry, construction
and wood pulp industries. A tall tree, the
Norway Spruce can be over 30 m high with a
trunk of 1.5 m in diameter.

WINDBREAKS, HEDGES
AND SHELTER FOR BIRDS
W.T. Macoun stated in 1924 that the Norway
Spruce is a good choice for windbreaks and
hedges. He was right; trees that are now over
100 years old can be found in the eastern
Windbreak that starts at the magnolia collection
and extends toward Dow's Lake. Earlier, in
1897, Macoun wrote, "…the Norway Spruce
makes a compact, firm, handsome hedge and
is ornamental at all seasons of the year but, as
it is a very vigorous grower, it requires severer
clipping than some others…"

A hedge of this species can be found in the
Ornamental Gardens. Spruce foliage and twigs
have little nutrition for wildlife, but dense
crowns provide good shelter and seeds for birds
and small mammals. Non-lethal fungi damage
to needles and twigs is common. Mites have
been reported as a major problem and pest
control may be required in hot dry summers.

Immature cones (above) grow upright initially. They hang down when mature. Mature bark (below) has small, rounded scales.

Conical-shaped crowns are dense almost to the ground (above).

Needles are short, rigid and rectangular in cross-section, remaining on drooping twigs for up to 7 years as new growth (left) appears.

Salix alba
WHITE WILLOW

Narrow leaves have dark outer and light inner surfaces. Bright yellow twigs are noticeable in early spring.

The tree builds a vast, oval-shaped crown and a massive, short trunk in a few decades.

k.gier

Willows are perhaps the most recognizable of all trees, especially the graceful Weeping Willows, yet it is difficult to identify the various species. Their differences are obscure and there are many hybrids. About 250 species of willow can be found in the northern hemisphere, of which 75 to 90 are native to North America.

The Arboretum contains over 30 species and varieties of willow, most of them in the willow area near Dow's Lake and the small island. A mature White Willow grows on the slope down from the Eastern Lookout and willow hedges can be seen in the old hedge collection in the Campus area.

CONTROLS SHORELINE EROSION

The natural habitat of the White Willow is next to rivers in Europe and northern Asia. It is among the first trees to grow on fresh sedimentary deposits or eroded banks of rivers. Willows have often been planted to combat shoreline erosion. They can be washed away in floods and have a short life in woodlands where they are replaced by alders or elms.

There is great ornamental value in the slender leaves and rugged bark of the White Willow and its many cultivars, all of which are popular for landscaping projects near water. The White Willow is a large shade tree with wide-spreading branches, pendulous at the tips. Its wood is light and soft, with limited uses, whereas young sprouts are excellent for basketry and furniture making.

Bees and other insects feed on the early spring nectar produced by White Willows. The tree is not susceptible to serious diseases or pests, although heart rot fungi will often decompose the boles of old trees and make hollow trunks prone to damage by wind or snow.

Male and female flowers (catkins) grow on separate trees and need bees or other insects to cross pollinate. Later in the summer, capsules open to release small woolly seeds.

White Willow bark is thick and coarse because of deep furrows and short irregular ridges.

fyi Salix comes *from the Celtic* sal-lis, *meaning* *"near water".*

ARBORETUM WALKS

Six walks are suggested to view the selected trees and as an introduction to the collection of about 4,000 trees and shrubs. Distances are short, allowing time to combine walks and to meander, ponder and picnic.

WALK A Circle

WALK B Maple

WALK C Windbreak

WALK D Two Bridges

WALK E Southern

WALK F Campus

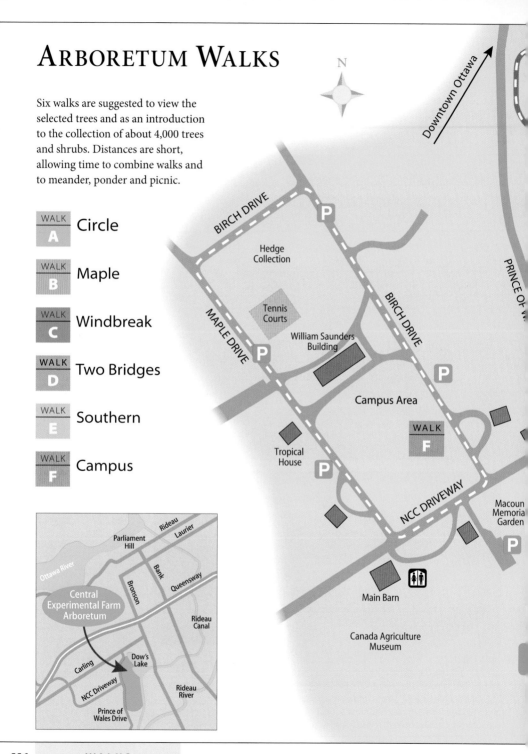

N

Downtown Ottawa

BIRCH DRIVE

Hedge Collection

Tennis Courts

MAPLE DRIVE

William Saunders Building

BIRCH DRIVE

PRINCE OF W

Campus Area

WALK F

Tropical House

NCC DRIVEWAY

Macoun Memorial Garden

Main Barn

Canada Agriculture Museum

Ottawa River

Parliament Hill

Rideau

Laurier

Bank

Bronson

Queensway

Central Experimental Farm Arboretum

Rideau Canal

Carling

Dow's Lake

NCC Driveway

Rideau River

Prince of Wales Drive

Magnolias

Old Windbreak

Dow's Lake

WALK
C

P

CIRCLE ROAD

ds
e Farm
ing 72

WALK
A

Eastern
Lookout

Hosta
Garden

Poplar Area

Circle Area

Woodlands

WALK
D

WALK
B

Maple Area

P Southern
Lookout

c
e

ental
ens

Little
Island

WALK
E

Windbreak

Rideau Canal

Oak Area

Elms and
Hackberries

CIRCLE WALK

- The Circle area is for meandering on the grass and discovering many of the oldest trees in the Arboretum.

- This is a flat area. The distance given is for the Circle Road which is paved and wheelchair accessible. The road is closed in winter.

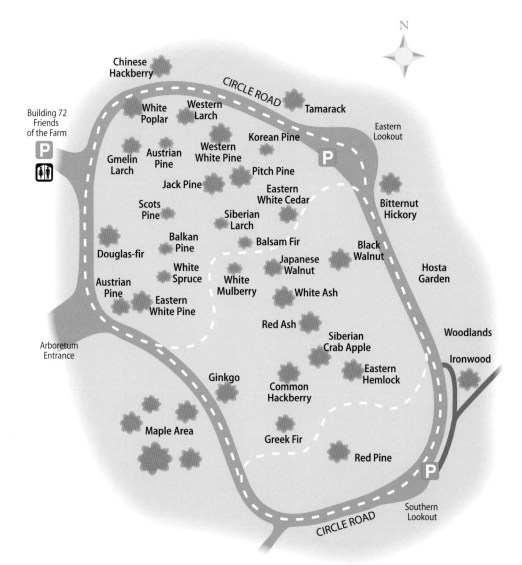

N

CIRCLE ROAD

Chinese Hackberry

Building 72
Friends
of the Farm
P

White Poplar

Western Larch

Tamarack

Eastern Lookout

Gmelin Larch

Austrian Pine

Western White Pine

Korean Pine

Pitch Pine

Jack Pine

Scots Pine

Eastern White Cedar

Siberian Larch

Bitternut Hickory

Balkan Pine

Balsam Fir

Black Walnut

Douglas-fir

Japanese Walnut

Hosta Garden

Austrian Pine

White Spruce

White Mulberry

White Ash

Eastern White Pine

Red Ash

Woodlands

Arboretum Entrance

Siberian Crab Apple

Ironwood

Ginkgo

Common Hackberry

Eastern Hemlock

Maple Area

Greek Fir

Red Pine

P

Southern Lookout

CIRCLE ROAD

MAPLE WALK

- South of the Circle road is the flat, grassed Maple Area. After exploring there, consider taking the Southern Walk.

- There are many interesting and beautiful shrubs in the area.

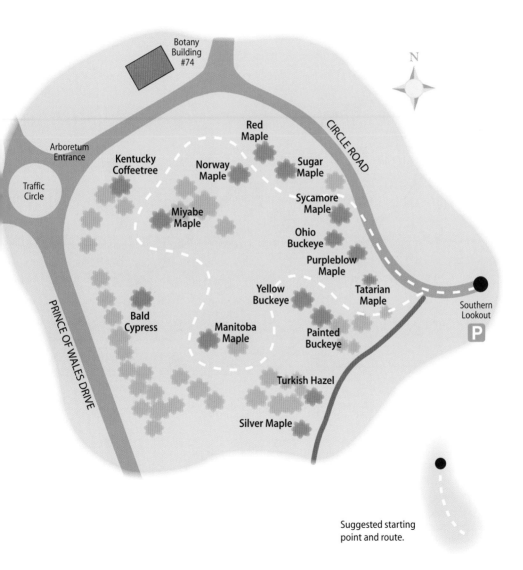

N

Botany Building #74

Arboretum Entrance

Traffic Circle

CIRCLE ROAD

Red Maple

Kentucky Coffeetree

Norway Maple

Sugar Maple

Miyabe Maple

Sycamore Maple

Ohio Buckeye

Purpleblow Maple

Yellow Buckeye

Tatarian Maple

Bald Cypress

Manitoba Maple

Painted Buckeye

Southern Lookout

P

PRINCE OF WALES DRIVE

Turkish Hazel

Silver Maple

Suggested starting point and route.

WINDBREAK WALK

- The return walk on the grass is steep.
- Dow's Lake is a short walk away from the southern end of the Windbreak.

- The old Windbreak of Ponderosa, Scots and Austrian Pines and Norway Spruce was established in 1895.

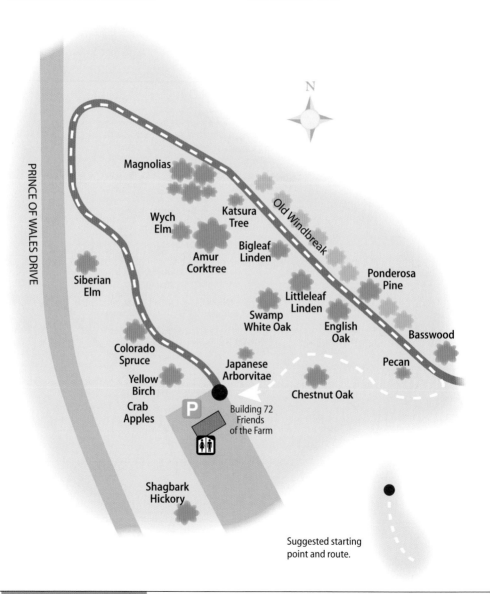

N

PRINCE OF WALES DRIVE

Magnolias

Wych Elm

Katsura Tree

Old Windbreak

Amur Corktree

Bigleaf Linden

Siberian Elm

Littleleaf Linden

Ponderosa Pine

Swamp White Oak

English Oak

Basswood

Colorado Spruce

Japanese Arborvitae

Pecan

Yellow Birch

Chestnut Oak

Crab Apples

P

Building 72
Friends of the Farm

Shagbark Hickory

Suggested starting point and route.

TWO BRIDGES WALK

- The path through the Woodlands is paved and steep. The entire walk is wheelchair accessible.
- Visit the Hosta Garden (not wheelchair accessible).

- South of this walk is a new windbreak of White and Red Pine, and White and Red Spruce.

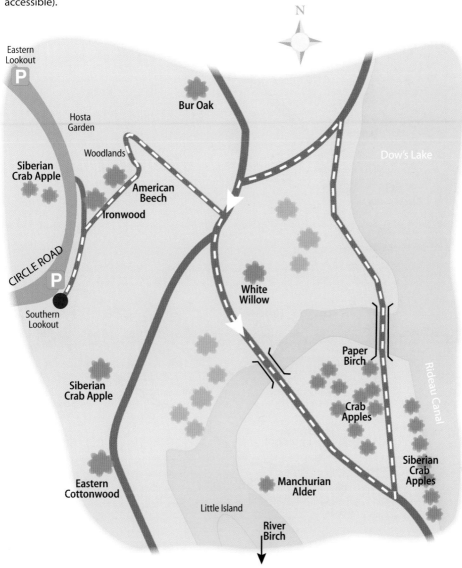

N

Eastern
Lookout
P

Bur Oak

Hosta
Garden

Woodlands

Dow's Lake

Siberian
Crab Apple

American
Beech

Ironwood

CIRCLE ROAD

P

Southern
Lookout

White
Willow

Paper
Birch

Siberian
Crab Apple

Crab
Apples

Rideau Canal

Siberian
Crab
Apples

Eastern
Cottonwood

Manchurian
Alder

Little Island

River
Birch

SOUTHERN WALK

- Slopes on the unpaved paths are gentle and wheelchair accessible.
- Near the southernmost bend in the path, there is an entrance to the Fletcher Wildlife Garden.

- Beyond the Northern Catalpas, the path to the south is lined with elms and hackberries, and a new collection of nut trees is on the eastern side.

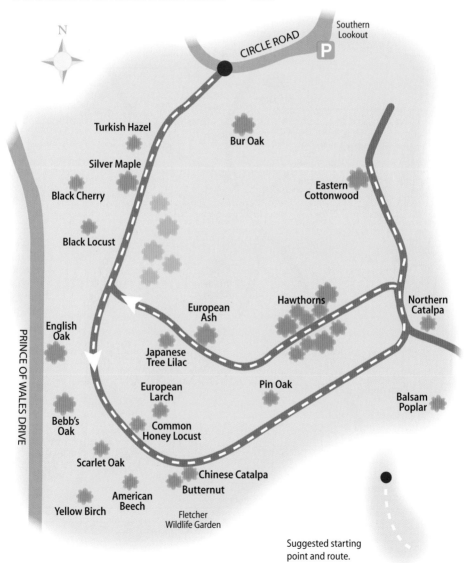

N

Southern Lookout

CIRCLE ROAD

P

Turkish Hazel

Bur Oak

Silver Maple

Eastern Cottonwood

Black Cherry

Black Locust

English Oak

European Ash

Hawthorns

Northern Catalpa

Japanese Tree Lilac

European Larch

Pin Oak

PRINCE OF WALES DRIVE

Bebb's Oak

Common Honey Locust

Balsam Poplar

Scarlet Oak

Chinese Catalpa

Butternut

Yellow Birch

American Beech

Fletcher Wildlife Garden

Suggested starting point and route.

CAMPUS WALK

WALK F — 1.0 KM

- This is an easy, flat walk and wheelchair accessible.
- The distance given is for the road loop. Feel free to wander on the lawns.

- After viewing the trees, visit the Macoun Memorial Garden, Ornamental Gardens, Tropical House, Canada Agriculture Museum.

GLOSSARY

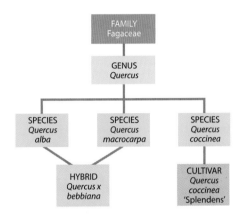

The Oak Family Tree (partial)

FAMILY TREE

Genus A group of closely related plant species.

Species A distinctive group of plants that naturally reproduce unique features over a number of generations.

Hybrid A plant growing from seeds produced as a result of cross pollination between different species.

Variety A plant which differs slightly from the species prototype. It occurs naturally or in cultivation.

Cultivar A plant variety that has been produced in cultivation by selective breeding; a cultivated variety.

LEAF LINGO

Terminal Growing at the end of a twig or branch.

Simple leaf A single leaf that grows on the tree as an individual unit.

Opposite Leaves and buds arranged in pairs, on opposite sides of twigs.

Alternate Single or compound leaves and buds at different (usually spiral) points on twigs.

Compound leaf A leaf composed of several leaflets attached to a common stalk.

Leaflet A leaf-like part of a compound leaf.

Palmate leaves The main veins of the leaf radiate from one point. No distinct midrib occurs.

Palmately compound leaves Having leaflets arising from one point.

Pinnately compound leaves Having leaflets, either opposite or alternate, arranged on either side of a common stem.

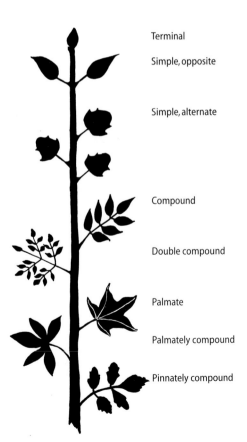

GLOSSARY CONTINUED

FLOWER FUNDAMENTALS

Pistil The female part of a flower that produces the seed and comprises the ovary, style and stigma.

Stamen The male part of a flower that bears pollen.

Anthers The part of the stamen of a flower that contains the pollen.

Sepals Small leaf-like structures which collectively make up the calyx, or outer envelope of a flower.

Perfect flower A flower that has both female (pistil) and male (stamen) organs. Usually, the flower shows radial symmetry.

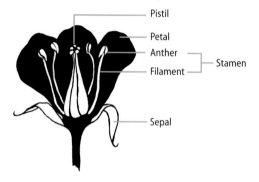

Pistil
Petal
Anther
Filament
Stamen
Sepal

OTHER TERMS

Arboretum A place where trees are grown for study and public display.

Bole The trunk of a tree.

Bottomland River valleys, in cross-section, usually comprise several elements. The lower part of a river valley, close to the watercourse and flooded often in spring or after heavy rains, is named the 'bottomland'.

Bract A leaf or petal-like structure occurring beneath a flower or fruit.

Catkin A long cluster of tiny male or female flowers.

Cones The dry fruit of a pine, fir or cedar tree, composed of stiff, overlapping, woody scales arranged spirally around an axis and enclosing seeds.

Conifer A plant that produces cones instead of flowers. It may be evergreen with needles, evergreen with scales, or deciduous. It may be either a tree or shrub.

Deciduous tree Tree that loses its leaves, unlike an evergreen.

Drupe A soft, fleshy fruit enclosing a hard-shelled seed.

Dwarf A plant that is stunted in its growth and often has abnormal proportions.

Forest glade Naturally occurring clearing in the woods.

Gland A surface or protuberance that secretes a substance.

Husk The outer covering of certain fruits, e.g. walnut.

Inflorescence A composite arrangement of flowers on the stem.

Lenticel A small, corky spot on the bark.

Native A tree produced, originated or grown in a particular region or country; indigenous.

Nectar A sugar-rich liquid secreted by glands of a plant to encourage pollination by insects and other animals. It is collected by bees to make into honey.

Needles Stiff, narrow leaves with linear veins, such as those of conifers.

Panicle A loose compound flower cluster (inflorescence) produced by irregular branching.

Pioneer A tree species which invades a site disturbed by natural or manmade catastrophes such as fire, hurricane, or clear-cutting.

Pod A long, dry fruit which splits to release seeds.

Riparian forests Forests which grow naturally on the sides or lower banks of watercourses; in wet areas where no stagnant water occurs.

Samara A winged, usually one seeded, fruit that does not split open, as of the maple. Also called a key.

Scales A thin covering of a bud or twig; also cone-scale (see Cones).

Spirals Branches or leaves circling around a central line to form a series of constantly changing planes.

Stand The growing trees in a forest or part of a forest.

Taproot The main root of a tree growing straight downward from the trunk.

Understorey A layer of vegetation beneath the main canopy of a forest. Usually, it consists of tall or low shrubs.

Weeping A tree having slender, drooping or pendulous branches.

Whorls A ring of branches growing at the same level around the tree trunk.

Windbreak One or a few rows of trees or shrubs, such as a hedge, that protects from or breaks the force of the wind.

BIBLIOGRAPHY

Agriculture & Agri-Food Canada (AAFC), formerly known as Department of Agriculture and Agriculture Canada

Appendix to the Report of the Minister of Agriculture, Experimental Farms Report, Government Printer, Ottawa, Annual Reports, 1887-1930; periodic reports, 1931-1954

Guide to the Central Experimental Farm, Dominion Experimental Farms, Government Printing Bureau, Ottawa, 1912

Fifty Years of Progress on Dominion Experimental Farms, 1886-1936, Government Printing Bureau, Ottawa, 1939

Anstey, T.H., *One Hundred Harvests: Research Branch, Agriculture Canada, 1886-1986*, Research Branch, Agriculture Canada, Horticulture Series No. 27, 1986

Barnard, Edward Sibley, *New York City Trees: A Field Guide for the Metropolitan Area*, City of New York Parks & Recreation, Columbia University Press, New York, 2002

Blouin, Glen, *An Eclectic Guide to Trees East of the Rockies*, Boston Mills Press, Erin, Ontario, 2001

Buck, F.E., *The Planting and Care of Shade Trees*, Department of Agriculture, Bulletin No. 19, Second Series, Government Printing Bureau, Ottawa, 1914

Buckley, A.R., *Trees and Shrubs of the Dominion Arboretum*, Research Branch, Agriculture Canada, Publication 1697, 1980

Buckley, A.R., *Garden Notes from the Plant Research Institute*, Department of Agriculture, November 16, 1964 – December 26, 1967; also *This Week in the Arboretum*, occasional from 1949

(The) Canadian Countryman, "Dr. William Saunders", Vol. 25, No. 25, June 20, 1936

Cole, Trevor J., *A Checklist of Ornamental Trees for Canada* (revision of 1968 edition by Lawrence C. Sherk), Canada Department of Agriculture, Ottawa Research Station, Ottawa, Ontario, Publication 1343, 1979

Cole, Trevor, *The Ontario Gardener*, Whitecap Books, Vancouver/Toronto, 1991

Davies, Blodwen, *Ottawa: Portrait of a Capital*, McGraw-Hill, 1954

Dore, W.G., "The Director's Wife Describes 'The Farm' 73 Years Ago," *Greenhouse-Garden-Grass 7*, no. 4, Winter 1968

Douglas, Brian, editor, *The Living Collection of the Dominion Arboretum*, Agriculture & Agri-Food Canada (AAFC), www.agr.gc.ca/sci/arboretum, 2005

Eastman, John, *The Book of Forest and Thicket: Trees, Shrubs, and Wildflowers of Eastern North America*, Stackpole Books, Harrisburg PA., 1992

Farrar, John Laird, *Trees in Canada*, Fitzhenry & Whiteside Limited and the Canadian Forestry Service of Natural Resources Canada, 1995

Hageneder, Fred, *The Meaning of Trees*, Chronicle Books, San Francisco, 2005

Harris, Julie & Jennifer Mueller, "Making Science Beautiful: The Central Experimental Farm, 1886-1939," *Ontario History*, Volume LXXXIX, Number 2, June 1997

Harris, Marjorie, *Botanica North America*, HarperCollins, New York, 2003

Hosie, R.C., *Native Trees of Canada*, 7th Edition, Canadian Forestry Service, 1969

Kershaw, Linda, *Trees of Ontario*, Lone Pine, Canada, 2001

Macoun, W.T., *Best Conifers Hardy at Ottawa*, in Canada Department of Agriculture, Ottawa, Ontario, Annual Report, 1924, pp 36-44

Macoun, W.T., *Best Ornamental Deciduous Trees Hardy at Ottawa*, in Canada Department of Agriculture, Ottawa, Ontario, Annual Report, 1925, pp 32-48

Oliver, R.W., *Trees for Ornamental Planting*, Canada Department of Agriculture, Ottawa, Ontario, Publication 995, 1959 (Reprint of 1957 edition)

Oxford Encyclopedia of Trees of the World, Peerage Books, London, 1981

Saunders, W. & W.T. Macoun, "Catalogue of the Trees and Shrubs in the Arboretum and Botanic Garden, at the Central Experimental Farm, Ottawa, Ontario, Canada", *Deparment of Agriculture Bulletin No. 2, Second Series*, Ottawa, June 1899

Silvics of North America: Vol. 1. Conifers; Vol. 2. Hardwoods, Agriculture Handbook 654, U.S. Department of Agriculture, Forest Service, Washington, D.C., 1990

Smith, H. and Bramley, M., *Ottawa's Farm: a History of the Central Experimental Farm*, General Store Publishing House, 1996

Index of Tree Names

About the Friends of the Central Experimental Farm

The Friends of the Central Experimental Farm (or the Friends of the Farm) is a volunteer organization with approximately 500 members and 250 active volunteers, all of whom support the mission of helping to protect and enhance this beautiful and historic green space in the heart of Ottawa, Canada's capital city.

In working with the staff of Agriculture and Agri-Food Canada, the Friends donate up to 15,000 hours of volunteer time throughout the year to help in the gardens and the Arboretum, to raise funds, to do research, to provide educational programs and special events, and to raise public awareness of this extraordinary place.

This book is one of many projects the Friends have undertaken since inception in 1988. Other achievements include: publishing the book "Ottawa's Farm", helping to restore the rose, peony, iris and daylily gardens, establishing a hosta garden, enhancement and promotion of the Farm's lilac collection, helping to get the Farm designated as a National Historic Site and Heritage Landscape, and providing 700 new trees through our Donor Tree Program.

Despite many successes, support through donations, membership and volunteer work is always needed. This gives the Friends a strong voice in advocacy and action to protect the Farm and enables the work at the Farm to continue.

Please help the Friends by making a donation, becoming a member, and/or becoming a volunteer. Your support is vital and much appreciated.

For more information on how you can help, contact Friends of the Farm, Building 72, The Arboretum, Central Experimental Farm, Ottawa, Ontario, Canada K1A 0C6. Tel: (613)230-3276; Fax: (613)230-1238; Email: info@friendsofthefarm.ca or visit the website www.friendsofthefarm.ca.